My MUSLIM Friends

PETER YOUNGREN

ISBN 1-895868-51-3

CONTENTS

INTRODUCTION

Welcome to "My Muslim Friends." First let me acknowledge that this book makes no pretense of an overall evaluation of Islam, the Koran or current events. It does not provide an analysis of terrorism or militant Islam. Many books that address these topics have already been written. My purpose is to show opportunities for friendship and dialogue between Muslims and Christians, and to highlight one question: who is Jesus?

Though my background gave me an attitude of suspicion towards those of non-Christian religions, I have come to recognize that people are people, with similar hopes, dreams and aspirations no matter where we live or what our cultural background is. Yes, there are extremists in Islam, but the vast majority of Muslims are peace-loving, hard-working people.

The title, "My Muslim Friends," expresses my sincere attitude towards Muslims and I often use these three words as I address audiences that include tens of thousands of Muslims in various parts of the world.

Friendship is a key to human relations. You can respect one another without being in agreement on a range of issues. The most prominent Gospel preacher of the first century, the apostle Paul, practiced this principle of "respect without compromise." Of course the apostle was merely walking in the footsteps of Jesus.

The reader will quickly discover that Jesus is the main topic of this book. He is a person of great interest to Christians as well as Muslims. The Bible as well as the Koran, Islam's holy book, give Jesus a supreme position. Who is this Jesus Christ, born of a virgin, sinless, the Messiah and the One who will return?

My hope is that this book will be a journey of discovery for both Christians and Muslims.

Finally a few words of gratitude. Thank you Dr. T. L. Osborn for opening my eyes to the power of the Gospel, when it is preached with signs, wonders and miracles.

Thank you to Aril Edvardsen of Norway. Your love for the world and your approach of friendship towards those of a non-Christian religion has been a great inspiration to me.

Thank you Emmanuel Luther Ratiq for your writings. You opened my understanding to the witness of Jesus in the Muslim culture.   - Peter Youngren

CHAPTER ONE

TAKE ANOTHER LOOK AT JESUS

Jesus is a point of contact between Muslims and Christians. The only ancient religious writings that give Jesus a supreme position are the Bible and Islam's holy book, the Koran, which mentions Jesus ninety-seven times. Entire chapters are dedicated to Him. Though there are stark differences in how Christians and Muslims view Jesus, still without question He remains a person of common interest and a point of dialogue.

Let me be very clear where I stand. Jesus came for the world; no religion or culture owns Him. He loves the world, died for all, and rose again to give new life to everyone. His grace extends to all religions including Muslims and Christians alike. Jesus is the Savior of all people.

One of the first comments I make to Muslim friends is, *"I am not trying to convert you to Christianity."* That does not mean that I view Christianity in a negative light, though just like any religion, Christianity has its share of problems. It is just that no religion, no matter how well intentioned, has the power to make us righteous. That ability is in Jesus alone. For years I have endeavored to show Christians our need to receive new life through Jesus Christ. How we respond to Jesus is a crucial matter for every person regardless of religion. This is an area of complete equality; everyone, man or woman, Christian or

Muslim, rich or poor, who believes and receives God's love revealed in Jesus has eternal life.

My mission in life is to share this Good News of Jesus Christ. For thirty years I have enjoyed working with Christians of almost all denominations and in all parts of the world. Our common denominators are our love for people and our faith in the Gospel of Jesus Christ.

MUHAMMAD, THE KORAN AND CHRISTIANS

In addition to working with Christians, I gladly work with all people who promote peace and mutual understanding. My travels have brought me into contact with many Muslims who are honest, hard-working and peace-loving individuals. I have often received friendship and understanding from Muslims. It has been my joy to extend a hand of friendship to people of other religions than my own, according to the example given by Jesus and the apostle Paul, who refused to discriminate against any individual or groups of people. My friendship with Muslims has not caused me to compromise my belief in the Gospel. On the contrary it has helped me to really focus on the core of our message, which is Jesus and what He has done for the world. When we turn from self–righteousness and self-reliance and receive the Messiah sent from God into our hearts, we receive peace from God. Jesus Himself is our Prince of Peace.

I remember how shocked I was to discover that the Koran speaks highly of the Gospel. Islam's prophet Muhammad taught that the Gospel is from God, but millions of Muslims and Christians know little or nothing about the Gospel. This ignorance makes the task of presenting Christ's Good News to all people extremely urgent.

In the early days of Islam, Muhammad had a particularly good relationship with Christians. Christians and Jews are called by the Arabic term "Ahl al Kitab," meaning the "People of the Book." The Koran puts forth this idea of goodwill towards Ahl al Kitab: "You will find that the closest to you in love are those who call themselves Christians, because there are priests and monks among them who do not behave arrogantly" (Surah 5:83).

Muslims were encouraged to accept the Scriptures of Jews and Christians, and to live in peace with them. "And argue not with the People of the Book unless it be in (a way) that is better, save with such of them as do wrong; and say: We believe in that which has been revealed unto us and revealed unto you; our God and your God is One, and unto Him we surrender" (Surah 29:46).

The Koran goes as far as saying that if a Muslim has questions they can refer to the "People of the Book," "ask those who have been reading the Book before thee" (Surah 10:95).

During the later part of Muhammad's life the Koran records instances of hostilities between Muslims and Christians, as well as rebukes of Christians. Still the verses quoted above show openness and good-will. I would rather focus on common denominators, and on building bridges, than on that which engenders further strife. Enough books have been written about wars between Christians and Muslims. My focus is Jesus and His love extended to all.

I am very serious when I say I do not try to convert people from one religion to another. This would be fruitless since no religion is able to save even one person. Christians are sometimes offended when I make this statement. It is very easy for us Christians to put our focus on the religion of Christianity rather than the person of Jesus. A quick look at the Bible will reveal that salvation is not found in adherence to a religion. Statements from the Bible like: "he who has the Son (Jesus) has life" and eternal life is in "no other name than Jesus" put the focus squarely on Jesus and Jesus alone (more about this later).

While I do not try to convert people from one religion to another, I seek to influence people of all religions to embrace Jesus Christ and His righteousness, which is a free gift to all who believe. This is not all the same as trying to convert a person from one religion to another. In fact, millions claim adherence to Christianity, and still have no knowledge of the free gift of Jesus' righteousness.

SEPT 11, 2001 HARDENS ATTITUDES

We are living in a difficult world that seemingly inches ever closer to the precipice of disaster. Tension in the Middle East is a constant factor and people everywhere feel the threat of terrorism. I think most people would agree the attitudes towards Islam worldwide have hardened since September 11, 2001. Many books with a negative bias against Islam have been written by Christian authors. Words that engender fear and anger such as "unveiling," "de-masking," "dark side," "terrorism" and "jihad" are common in titles and subtitles. Unfortunately, many of the writers lack knowledge of Islam or the Koran. When one Christian leader heard I was writing a book about a friendship approach between Christians and Muslims his immediate response was, "No one will buy it." I understand his thinking, though I strongly disagree. To use the words "Muslim" and "friends" in the same sentence may indeed be politically incorrect to some.

The last few years we have been inundated, not only with

books, but television documentaries and newspaper articles attempting to analyze Islam and its followers. Some Christian ministers have ridiculed Islam and belittled Muslims, while showing an appalling ignorance of Islamic beliefs and of the Muslim world. I heard one Christian preacher rally people to military action, speaking of the "historical confrontation" between the Western world and Islam. His tone and rhetoric had a sense of violence and hatred to it. It reminded me of what we read in history about the Crusaders who fought for the city of Jerusalem almost nine hundred years ago. Those "Christian" armies were promised an instant entry into heaven if they died in battle. This kind of fanaticism has existed and does exist in every religion. It is not the way Jesus approached people.

STILL CRUSADING?

Some Christian writers have made it their aim to demonize Islam's prophet Muhammad. One well-known author claims the suicide bombings in the Middle East are expressions of "pent up sexual desires similar to those of the founder of Islam." These kinds of comments are not only baseless, but they serve only to enrage and alienate. Furthermore, this type of writing is unworthy of someone who claims to be a follower of Jesus. Those speaking of the "dark side" of Islam would do well to remember that dark sides can be found in many religions and philosophies including Christianity. The Crusader era exemplifies this dark side of Christianity.

Other Christian writers view every conflict only in the context of a Muslim conspiracy to take over the world. Regional wars in places like Chechnya, the Middle East and Kashmir are all viewed in this light with little or no consideration given to local conditions. One gets the distinct impression that the authors have never engaged in a serious conversation with Muslims or clerics of the Muslim religion. The tragic fact is that Mus-

11

lims have killed Christians and Christians have killed Muslims. In the Balkan war during the 1990's one of the atrocities was "Christians" killing Muslims in Kosovo. I put the word "Christian" in quotation marks because true followers of Jesus would not engage in genocide. When people kill in the name of Christianity it is to defend a tradition or an institution. This is not the spirit of Jesus Christ.

Many Christians have no idea that Jesus is mentioned far more in the Koran than Muhammad is. They don't know that Christians and Muslims have some beliefs in common. Sadly some Christians view Muslims as enemies and vice versa.

GOD IS LOVE

The basis for everything we know of God is that God is love. Any religion that drifts from this becomes dangerous. Without God's love religious teachings become lifeless words, which are full of condemnation. It doesn't matter which religion we speak of; words of condemnation always contain seeds of violence and hatred. On the contrary, wholesome religion reaches from the human heart toward a God full of love. When God's mercy, kindness and forgiveness touch people His love brings healing to the wounded human conscience. God's love becomes an instrument of restoration where division and strife have ruled.

Now a word to Muslims. In this book I ask you to take another look at who Jesus really is. The Bible has much to say about Jesus, but so does the Koran. *What does the Koran really say about Jesus?* Please, receive this book as an expression of love, care and respect. The last few years have been difficult for Muslims. Many have experienced discrimination and condescension, especially those living in Europe and North America. We see in the Bible that Jesus and the apostles never treated others with disrespect. Jesus reserved harsh words only for religious bigots while common people received grace, mercy and love. If you have been mistreated simply because you are a Muslim, please know there are millions of Jesus-followers, who exhibit the non-condemning spirit of Jesus (John 3:17).

It is not possible to write a book like this without addressing sensitive areas. It is not my intention to offend anyone, Christian or Muslim. My hope is that people of all religions, including Christians and Muslims, will discover Jesus in a greater way than ever before.

A word to Christians. Many will receive this book joyously praising God for the witness of Jesus in Muslim culture. Others may have a difficult time with some of the content. You may have listened to preaching that speaks in a condescending tone toward Muslims and you may think that I am too loving, too open or even compromising.

I hope you will see I am approaching this matter in the way that Jesus, the apostle Paul and the other disciples did. The Biblical record is clear that true believers in Jesus do not speak in a derogatory manner regarding other religions. We are not people of condemnation, but of Good News! Our focus is sharing the love of God as it is revealed in Jesus Christ.

A word about the Koran. All quotations are from well-respected English translations of the Koran. Some may suggest that since the Koran was recorded in Arabic, it is only understood by those who speak Arabic. I am sure legitimate arguments can be made as to the exact meaning of words in Arabic compared to English. In any translation from one language to another nuances can be lost and I'm sure this may also be the case with the English version of the Koran. At the same time, I am encouraged to know that the English translations of the Koran have been done by esteemed Islamic scholars whose intent has been to give as exact a translation as is possible. Further the Koran itself claims to be a message to all people, so it would seem inherent that its message should be comprehensible to all including those whose native tongue is not Arabic.

May the following chapters provide for opportunities of dialogue. For Christians who have never thought of Muslims as friends, I pray your heart will be opened as you see those outside of the Christian religion in a fresh light. God loves the world. For Muslims and Christians I pray that you will discover Jesus in a greater way than ever before.

CHAPTER TWO

FRIENDSHIP OPENS DOORS

Are Christianity and Islam on an inevitable collision course? If you follow the news it is hard to avoid hearing inflammatory remarks by extremists. Words that fuel anger are hurled from all sides. Muslims protest against Christians and Christians are just as vehement in their verbal attacks. Insults and condescension are not Jesus' way, nor does such an approach reveal God's love. Jesus found a way over two thousand years ago to share God's love with Jews, Samaritans and Romans, in spite of the fact that each of these groups carried their own set of prejudices and suspicions. Jesus did not discriminate between people. His love reached all cultures and cut through centuries of bitterness and hatred. His way can and will work today.

Islam's holy book, the Koran, speaks about Jesus' birth, teachings, miracles, ascension to heaven and His Second Coming. The Bible is divided into chapters and verses. In the Koran, chapters are called "surahs." Jesus is mentioned in fifteen surahs and ninety-three verses. Three surahs are specifically named after references to Jesus (Surah 3, 5, and 19).

While there is no denying a few stark disagreements between Islam and Christianity concerning Jesus; likewise, there is also no denying the many points of agreement. If there are any people outside of the Christian religion with whom it is easy to talk about Jesus, it is Muslims. Today, roughly 1.4 billion Muslims live, not only in the Middle East, but also in Indonesia, India, Pakistan, across Africa and virtually every nation of the world including North America and Europe. If God loves the world, and He does, Muslims are certainly included in His love. This calls for friendship.

THE WISE MAKE FRIENDS

Solomon said, "A man who has friends must himself be friendly" (Proverbs 18:24), and "He who wins souls is wise" (Proverbs 11:30). This is our approach! We build bridges of trust and friendship. My Muslim friends know I do not hide our differences. Yet, when I share my convictions about Jesus Christ, I do so with respect toward others in the same way the Apostle Paul spoke to people of other religions in the Roman world.

At times, when I'm about to conduct a Gospel Festival in a Muslim area Christians tell me, "You can't preach Jesus Christ there, the Muslims will stop you." Often these statements are nothing but fear mongering. In fact, Muslims have often received me with open arms. At the same time, there are areas of the world where a Gospel meeting will not be granted permission by the government. *I appeal to countries like Saudi Arabia, Yemen, Libya and Syria to allow for the Gospel to be heard.*

DIALOGUE AND THE KORAN

The Koran itself encourages an approach where each person is free to choose: "There is no forcing of anyone into this way of life. The truth stands clear from falsehood" (Surah 2:257). Some translations read, "Let there be no compulsion in religion." The Koran is positive towards dialogue with other religions. Muhammad often engaged in this practice with both

Jews and Christians. In his book "Understanding Islam," Iman Yahiya Emerick writes: "Islam...must support all religions. The Islamic government is forbidden to seize the churches, synagogues, or temples from any group, nor can the government meddle in the appointments of religious leaders by any group. The treaty Muhammad made with a local Christian community is very clear: No bishop can be removed from his office and no church can be confiscated."

Our approach of friendship towards Muslims has opened new doors. I have conducted large Gospel Festivals in cities where more than ninety-five percent of the population is Muslim. It had never been done and people told me it could never be done. Was it without difficulties and obstacles? No! Many prejudices had to be removed, but as I expressed friendship, while sharing God's love for all people revealed through Jesus' death and resurrection, doors opened.

I make it unequivocally clear that I will not criticize Islam. Why should I? The great apostle Paul never criticized the various religions and beliefs he encountered. He had too many positive things to say about Jesus Christ to take time for condescending words toward others. In his messages in Athens, Corinth, Ephesus and a host of other cities, there was never a hint of argument or condescension.

One example is in the city of Ephesus where the goddess Diana was worshipped. Even non-believers acknowledged that Paul had not spoken derogatory words about the religion of Ephesus. We read, "...these men...are neither robbers of temples nor blasphemers of your goddess" (Acts 19:37). If the apostle Paul did not take time to criticize a Roman goddess how much less should I as a believer in Jesus criticize Muslims who, after all, believe in the Supreme Almighty God? No, my focus is like Paul's: to show the love of God revealed through Jesus.

17

Solomon said it wisely, "The wise person makes friends." In a world of animosity, let's follow the approach of Jesus and Paul. Let's make friends.

WHAT FOOLS DO

"Any fool can start a quarrel." Solomon spoke these words and they hold true today. It's easy to stir up a fight or to make people angry. Speak condescending words, yell, argue, desecrate sacred symbols of other religions, and you will have a fight on your hands.

Solomon continues, "An angry man stirs up strife, and a furious man abounds in transgression" (Proverbs 29:22). Also, "A fool vents all his feelings, but a wise man holds them back" (Proverbs 29:11). All too often Christians and Muslims alike have vented their negative feelings. We look for whatever wrong we can find and make these wrongs our focus. I choose to focus on individuals with needs, and the urgency to share the message of Jesus with everyone.

MEET JESUS FIRST

Sharing Christ's Gospel has nothing to do with winning an argument. No one has ever experienced new life in Jesus Christ by winning or losing a debate. The new life that Christ offers comes by a miracle Jesus called being "born again." "Unless one is born again, he cannot see the kingdom of God" (John 3:3). To be born again, one must first meet Jesus. This does not happen by our own effort or reasoning. Jesus Christ Himself imparts His righteousness, redemption and new life into each person who is willing to receive. This makes arguments and demagoguery about religion fruitless.

My approach is to avoid debates about which religion is better, or even which holy book is superior to another. Jesus reminded us that we do not have eternal life in the scriptures, but in Him (John 5:39-40). Jesus Himself is eternal life. A mere discussion about which holy book is accurate and true is insufficient. There must be an encounter with Jesus. The Gospel is not about a set of beliefs that we accept mentally and academically. It is about meeting Jesus. The pattern is clear in the New Testament. People did not receive salvation by a careful study of Jesus' doctrines. No, they first had an encounter with Jesus and after this life-changing encounter, new believers had an appetite to learn the teachings of Jesus. First they met the Savior, and then came the doctrine of salvation. When Christ by His Spirit indwells a person, in time all other issues are settled. This miracle of Jesus Christ indwelling people is the heart and core of the Gospel (Colossians 1:27).

JUDGING OTHERS NOT ALLOWED

When some Christians hear me speak with kindness toward Muslims, they think I am compromising Christian ideals. How could I be? Jesus is our role model. We cannot be "more Christian" than Jesus. Two thousand years ago He demonstrated compassion without prejudice. The Jews would have preferred if Jesus had avoided the Samaritans. Similarly the Samaritans would have preferred if Jesus had shown prejudice against the Jews. Walls of division and hatred had separated these groups for centuries. Jesus touched all groups. He is our Savior and we walk in His footsteps. Jesus did not come to condemn people, but to save the world (John 3:16-17).

If love was Jesus' method, shouldn't it be ours? We do not condemn people; we bring the Good News of Jesus and leave the judgment of people to God. The apostle Paul forbids us from judging an outsider. Ultimately each person will be judged according to the Gospel, but that judgment is not for us to pronounce (John 12:47-48).

JUDGMENT: PAST AND FUTURE

Though I will address God's judgement of sin in more detail in the chapter entitled, "Grace, Not Law" let's look briefly at the word, as it relates to God, sin and eternity.

Judgment #1: The judgment for our sins and the sins of the whole world has already been given. Jesus took the judgment we deserved for our sins on Himself on the cross. Our sins have been punished and the punishment fell on Jesus (Isaiah 53:1-6, 1 John 12:31).

Judgment # 2: There is a "judgment to come." In this final judgment the world will be judged according to what each person has done with what Jesus did for us (Romans 2:16). The determining factor is whether we believed the Good News of what Jesus did and were saved by faith, or if we did not believe and are condemned (Mark 16:15).

Judgment # 3: This is a judgement of rewards for the works done "in the body" by those who believe in Jesus. Everyone at this judgement is already saved, and the basis for the judgement is the motivation for what we did. Those whose works are motivated by the indwelling Christ, works that Paul describes as "gold, silver and precious stones," will be rewarded. Others, whose works were religious in nature, and yet motivated by selfishness, vain ambition and other carnal reasons, will not be rewarded. The apostle Paul calls these works "wood, hay and stubble" (1 Corinthians 3:11-15). The book of Hebrews describes our own religious performance as "dead works" (Hebrews 6:1). This is in contrast to what believers do because they love God and are compelled by that love.

Simply put, judgment #1 is past, while judgment #2 and #3 are still to come.

FRIENDSHIP, NOT RIOT

Like many Christians, I grew up in an environment where Muslims were mistrusted. Somehow the idea reached my young mind that Muslims wanted to kill Christians. While there is no question that fanatical Muslims have killed Christians, it is equally true that fanatical Christians have killed Muslims.

Have my contacts with Muslims been without confrontation or conflict? By and large, yes. There have been a few occasions when tension or conflict erupted, but each time it was because Muslims erroneously thought that I was about to attack their religion.

Why would some Muslims think I wanted to speak against their religion? Let me explain. For more than thirty years I have conducted large Gospel Festivals around the world. Crowds of up to 600,000 have attended a single service. While not all the events reach that magnitude, almost all Festivals reach tens of thousands. It is impossible to conduct events on this scale without attracting attention from the media. On a few occasions Muslims have reacted negatively to our advertisements. On every occasion when I spoke with the Muslims who had opposed our event, I discovered the problem was based on their previous encounters with Christian preachers. They had heard Christian ministers who used the pulpit to belittle Islam and Muslims. When they saw our program advertised they assumed this was another event where Christians would bash Muslims.

I remember one tense occasion where rioting occurred in the streets before our Festival started. After the people heard my first message of Jesus they understood that I was not criticizing Islam. Fifteen Muslim leaders came late one night to my hotel. One by one these leaders asked my forgiveness. It was one of the most touching moments in my life when they said, "Mr. Youngren, we recognize now that you did not come to attack us or our religion, but you have only spoken lovingly about the Lord Jesus Christ."

When I was able share about God's love revealed in Jesus with an attitude of friendship, the misunderstandings were removed. I do not mean that we agreed on every fact, or that those Muslim leaders received Jesus as their Savior that night. No, we still had differences. However, when I focused on God's love revealed in Jesus there was a willingness to listen.

CARTOONS

In early 2006, European newspapers released cartoons of the prophet Muhammad. Muslims viewed these as blasphemous and demonstrations erupted across the world. Sadly, some died as a result of the protests. Christians vigorously defended the cartoons on the basis of freedom of the press. Muslim clerics were equally vigorous in calling the depictions blasphemous. Again many Christian preachers got in the fray. Some claimed that the violent demonstrations showed the true face of Islam. I cherish the western freedom of expression and sadly, this freedom is lacking in many Muslim countries. Still, Christians should know better than to attack other religions. When the media desecrates Christian values, we are offended and ask for it to be stopped. Christians protest movies like, "The Last Temptation of Christ" and "The DaVinci Code" because they portray Jesus in a way that is blasphemous to us. It should be natural for us to show respect for others. Our real task is far more important than to defend or criticize a cartoon. Politicians deal in politics. Newspaper editors deal in editorials.

Our concern is not freedom to speak ill against others, but freedom to express the good news of what God has done in Jesus Christ for the world. I challenge Christians to focus on our task, and I challenge Muslims to not be afraid to let the Gospel of Jesus Christ be heard.

AM I NAIVE?

To Christians who may consider me naive to propose friendship with Muslims in a world of violence and terrorism I ask, "How is your approach to the Muslim world working?" I question my Christian friends who attack and speak condescending words about Islam, "What results are you seeing?"

Most importantly, what is Jesus' approach? Jesus said, "If anyone hears My words and does not believe, I do not judge him; for I did not come to judge the world but to save the world. He who rejects Me, and does not receive My words, has that which judges him - the word that I have spoken will judge him in the last day" (John 12:47-48). These are amazing statements.

Jesus says:

1. He will not now judge the one who does not believe Him;
2. The purpose now is to bring salvation to people; and
3. Judgment will come in the last day.

Do you see how this frees us from judging others? This does not mean that there will never be a judgment. No, God will judge everyone on the last day.

There are many opportunities today to be drawn into political debates. Jesus also faced this challenge. The Samaritan woman who conversed with Jesus tried to get an argument started as to whether the correct place of worship was in the city of Jerusalem or in Samaria (John 4). The disciples wanted to discuss the establishment of the political kingdom of Israel (Acts 1:4-8). On each occasion, Jesus ignored the question and stayed focused on His message – to bring salvation and new life to all without discrimination. Jesus had not come to condemn, but to save. We follow Jesus!

CHAPTER THREE

JESUS IN THE KORAN

"The Bible or the Koran – Which One Leads to Paradise?" is a popular topic of debate. Such debates can be profitable, but they are often difficult. Why? Shockingly to many, the Bible clearly states that it does <u>not</u> lead to paradise. Jesus told the Pharisees in no uncertain terms that they were erroneous in thinking that they had eternal life in the scriptures (John 5:39).

Eternal life is not found in a book, but in a person. That person is Jesus Christ Himself who said, "I am the way, the truth, and the life. No one comes to the Father except through Me" (John 14:6). The apostle Peter stated, "There is no other name under heaven given among men by which we must be saved" (Acts 4:12).

If the concern is eternal life then knowledge of sacred literature is insufficient; Jesus is the only hope. The Bible is crucially important, because it is our source of information about what Jesus did and said. It may surprise many Christians that many important facts about Jesus, which are recorded in the Bible, are also in the Koran.

As I have already stated, there are differences of beliefs concerning Jesus between Muslims and Gospel believers. Notice I use the expression "Gospel believers." I make a distinction between Gospel believers and nominal Christians. Sadly, there are bishops and archbishops in major Christian denominations, who deny Jesus' virgin birth, His miracles and His Second Coming, while the Koran testifies of these things. Isn't it strange that in some ways we, who are Gospel believers, have more in common with Muslims than we have with some "Christian" leaders? That alone is cause for increased contact between Muslims and Gospel believers. If we who are Gospel believers find reason to dialogue with the denominational Christian leaders who deny many of the cardinal truths of Jesus, should we not also find grace in our hearts to treat Muslims with respect?

Let us for a moment lay aside our differences and look at what we have in common concerning Jesus. The following list of observations is based entirely on what the Koran says about Jesus. Christians may be shocked by these facts, while practicing Muslims probably have some knowledge already about these verses in the Koran. Take another look at Jesus. Who is He? Why does the Koran give Jesus this supreme position?

- Jesus was born of a virgin (Surah 19:16-27, Surah 21:92).

- Jesus is called the son of Mary (Surah 19:35). The angel Gabriel announced Jesus' supernatural birth. (Surah 3:43-46). The Bible states that the Holy Spirit would overshadow Mary and bring about the birth of Jesus. The Koran uses a similar expression in Surah 66:12, "And Mary daughter of Imran, whose body was chaste, therefore We breathed therein something of Our Spirit...." Why was Jesus' birth unique and different from all the other prophets?

- The Koran states that Mary was chosen and purified above all women of all nations (Surah 3:43). No other

26

woman is spoken of in these terms, not even Muhammad's mother, Lady Aminah, his wives or his daughters. Why is Mary singled out for such accolades? What made her supreme among women?

• The Koran recognizes Jesus had no earthly father unlike the other prophets, including Muhammad, whose father's name was Abdullah. Why is Jesus without an earthly father? Why is this unique position given to Jesus alone?

• Jesus is called "the word of God" (Surah 3:46, Surah 4:172). No other prophet is given this title. Others are called prophets of God, mouthpieces of God or messengers of God but never the word of God. It is one thing to be a messenger from God, speaking the word of God, while it is a whole other matter to be the word of God itself. Why is this exalted position reserved for Jesus? One cannot help but notice the similarity with the Gospel of John which states about Jesus, "In the beginning was the Word, and the Word was with God, and the Word was God...and the Word became flesh and dwelt among us, and we beheld His glory, the glory as of the only begotten of the Father, full of grace and truth" (John 1:1, 14);

• The Koran calls Jesus the "Messiah" (Surah 4:172; 9:31; 3:46; 5:73). Most language scholars agree that the Arabic word "al-masih" is directly related to the word "Messiah" which means "the Anointed One." No other prophet is given such high acclaim, not even Muhammad. Again we wonder why Jesus is given this unique position. Is this not further reason to look even deeper at who Jesus is? What is a Messiah? This title may need further examination. Jesus' own claims go beyond this Jewish nation; His message is for "everyone," "the world," even "the uttermost parts of the world." Out of the ninety-seven references to Jesus in

27

the Koran, eleven use the title "Al-Masiha-Isa." What does this mean? Why is Jesus given this supreme title?

• Jesus was empowered by the Holy Spirit (Surah 2:88);

• The Koran says Jesus will be held in honor in this world and the world hereafter (Surah 3:46);

• Jesus is sinless. He is never seen in a position where He had to ask for forgiveness of sin, such as the other prophets did. Instead, Jesus is without sin and protected from the evil one (Surah 3:37). Meanwhile, there are several references to Muhammad asking forgiveness for his sins (Surah 40:55). Muslims revere Adam, Noah, Abraham, and Moses as prophets and yet according to the Koran, they all had to seek pardon for their sins (Surah 3:147, 48:1-2);

• Jesus performed miracles (Surah 5:110-113). Most Muslims agree that Muhammad never performed any miracles. Some have tried to attribute miracles to Muhammad, but there is no such record in the Koran. Muhammad himself stated that if there was any further claim made regarding him outside of those found in the Koran, they should not be considered true. When questioned as to why he did not have any miracles, Muhammad told the people repeatedly that he was only a "warner and a guide." Muhammad disclaimed all power to work miracles (Surah 17:59, 29:49-50);

• The Koran says that Jesus will come back on the Day of Judgment (Surah 4:159).

WHY IS JESUS SINLESS?

Of all these remarkable statements about Jesus in the Koran,

JESUS IS SINLESS (as recorded in the Koran)

Adam sinned "Our Lord! We have wronged ourselves. If then Thou forgive me not and have mercy on me, surely we are lost." (Surah 7:23)

Abraham sinned "Forgive me my sin on the Day of Judgement" (Surah 26:83)

Moses sinned "My Lord! Lo! I have wronged my soul, so forgive me! (Surah 28:16)

David sinned "and he sought forgiveness of his Lord... and repented" (Surah 38:24)

Muhammad sinned "ask forgiveness for thy sin..." (Surah 47:19)

JESUS NEVER SINNED!

one of the most outstanding is that He is sinless. The whole idea of the Gospel is that only someone who is sinless can bring freedom to sinful humanity.

One sinner cannot take the punishment for another sinner anymore than one thief can go to prison on behalf of another thief. The Gospel claims that Jesus, by His death on the cross became our sin-bearer. When the Koran and the Bible claim that Jesus is sinless, this makes His death for our sins meaningful. Many have never pondered or explored this unique significance of Jesus and what it means.

What is the real meaning of the characteristics the Koran ascribes to Jesus? Here are some questions that might need a further examination.

Why was Jesus the only prophet born of a virgin? If His birth was a sign from God, as the Koran states, why was Jesus the only prophet to enjoy such a sign? Could it be that His purpose to redeem humanity from sin made the virgin birth necessary? If Jesus had an earthly father just like the other prophets, then we could immediately dismiss the idea that Jesus is the Savior of mankind. After all a mere human could not be the Savior of humanity.

WHO DECIDED JESUS' BLOOD-TYPE?

The Koran's testimony that Jesus was born of a virgin is a powerful statement, and it corroborates the idea that Jesus is the redeemer of mankind. The blood of Jesus carries enormous significance. The Gospel tells us that His blood is the very price paid for our salvation and that we who were far from God because of our sins have been brought near to God by the blood of Jesus. If Jesus' blood indeed carries such power, then it must be different from the blood of anyone else.

Interestingly, it is the father who determines the blood type of a child. The egg in the womb of a woman contains no blood. When a man and a woman have sexual relationship the blood type of the baby is determined by a genetic code when the egg is fertilized. The baby's blood never mingles with the mother's blood; they have two completely separate blood streams. A child can have a different blood type than either one of the parents. A mother can have Rh positive blood and the baby Rh negative. The mother's blood supports the unborn through the placenta, but her blood never enters the veins of the baby.

The genetic code of Jesus' blood was determined not by Mary, but by His Heavenly Father; Jesus' blood never mingled with Mary's. The egg in Mary's womb was fertilized without human involvement as both the Bible and the Koran testify. There was no sexual relationship involved in His birth. Instead the Holy Spirit overshadowed Mary, so that blood flowing through Jesus' veins would be divine. Human blood has been spilt throughout history, but it has not redeemed anyone. For Jesus' blood to be the agent of cleansing from all sins it had to be uniquely divine.

A baby inherits blood group factors at conception. Medical science claims there are 15 major blood types with an infinite number of combinations. Sophisticated DNA testing has determined that every single human has unique blood. Our blood, like our fingerprint, is uniquely ours. Jesus did not inherit a multiplicity of blood group factors from an earthly father and an earthly ancestry. When God's Spirit overshadowed Mary, the blood created in Jesus' unborn body was divine and uncontaminated by sin. Without this Jesus' blood would have been like any other, but now it has the power to save from sin.

JESUS AND ADAM

Some Muslims may wonder if this puts Jesus on the same level as Adam, who also did not have an earthly father, or for that matter an earthly mother. No, Jesus is superior to Adam in every way. The Bible puts it succinctly, "The first man [Adam] was of the earth, made of dust; the second man is the Lord from heaven" (1 Corinthians 15:47).

Notice these facts about Adam;
      ....he was created,
      ....he was from the earth,
      ....he was made of dust,
      ....he sinned.

None of these characteristics apply to Jesus. While Adam was created, Jesus was not. Instead a unique term, "only begotten" is used in the Bible in reference to Jesus' coming to earth. Later in this chapter we will look more at the phrase, "only begotten" and how it makes Jesus distinct.

Being both born of a virgin and sinless is a powerful combination. First Jesus' blood was uncontaminated by earthly forces, and then His life was protected from all evil and sin. Jesus is the perfect One. Isn't this a powerful indication of Jesus' purposes? In order to take the sins of the world on Himself, He had to be sinless, and to be sinless He has to be born of a virgin.

MUHAMMAD AND CHRISTIANS

It is astounding for non-Muslims to note the absence of great miracle claims about Muhammad in the Koran. Muhammad saw himself as a 'warner' and a 'guide,' a human in need of God's forgiveness. God commands Mohammed to "ask forgiveness for thy sin and for believing men" (Surah 47:19). Muhammad made no claim of miracles.

As noted in a previous chapter, early in his preaching Muhammad speaks of both Christians and Jews in a positive way calling them by the Arabic term "Ahl al-Kitab," which literally means "People of the Book." This phrase not only describes Christians and Jews, but it refers respectfully to the sacredness of the Bible. The Koran states: "The (Jews and Christians), we believe in the Revelation which has come down to us (the Koran) and in that which has come down to you [the Torah and the Gospels]" (Surah 29:46).

Muhammad encourages Muslims to get to know the "Gospels." Sadly, today many Christians as well as Muslims have little or no knowledge of the Gospels which is the Good News of Jesus Christ. Later on in his life Muhammad fought wars, including battles with both Jewish and Christian communities. These wars have been described in many books. Still the admonition remains in the Koran for Muslims to get to know the Gospel of Jesus Christ.

THE CROSS

Jesus' death on the cross and resurrection from the dead is a point of disagreement between Christians and Muslims. The fact that Jesus died on the cross and rose from the dead on the third day is fundamental to everything that is the Gospel and true Christianity. The apostle Paul expressed it this way, "I delivered to you first of all that which I also received: that Christ died for our sins according to the Scriptures" (1 Corinthians 15:3).

The commonly held belief among Muslims is that Jesus did not die on the cross, but was taken up to heaven by God. Some Muslims suggest that Judas was on the cross and that the Romans did not realize who they had crucified. I urge Muslims to consider that Jesus' death and resurrection are well-documented historical facts. It would not have been possible for the Gospel writers to add to the Gospel or to embellish them. They could not simply have made up the stories of the crucifixion and the resurrection. Had they done so, there would have been numerous records of those who contradicted the Biblical writers. Simply put, why is there no contemporary literature that contradicts these fantastic claims of Jesus' death, resurrection and ascension to heaven? Could it be that to contradict something which had been seen by hundreds of credible witnesses would have been intellectual suicide?

SURAH 19:34

There is an interesting reference in the Koran, Surah 19:34, where Jesus is quoted as saying, "Peace is on me the day I was born, the day that I die, and the day that I shall be raised up to life again." Look at this remarkable verse.

1. Jesus says that peace was upon Him the day He was born;

2. Jesus says that peace was upon Him the day He died;

3. Jesus says that peace was upon Him the day He was raised up to life again.

The birth, death and resurrection of Jesus are all summarized in one verse. Notice the sequence; Jesus was born, died and raised back to life again. This reminds me of the words of the apostle Paul in Romans 10:9, "If you confess with your mouth the Lord Jesus and believe in your heart that God has raised Him from the dead, you will be saved."

In another part of the Koran we read, "And the unbelievers plotted and planned, and Allah too planned, and the best of planners is Allah. 'Behold!' Allah said: 'O Jesus, I will take thee and raise thee to Myself and clear thee of the falsehood of those who blaspheme'" (Surah 3:55). Bible-believing Christians will have no problem with these verses from the Koran.

DID JESUS DIE ON THE CROSS?

Surah 4:157 is sometimes quoted as proof from the Koran that Jesus did not die on the cross, "But they said and boast, 'We killed Christ Jesus, the son of Mary, the apostle of Allah,' but they neither killed him nor crucified him, but so it was made to appear to them and those who differ therein are full of doubts with no certain knowledge, but only conjecture to follow for assurety they killed him not." This verse is a reference to the Jews, which is clearly seen in the context of Surah 4. Notice the words, "so it was made to appear to them." In other words, all appearances pointed towards the idea that the Jews had killed Jesus, but in fact it was not so.

While the Koran clearly states that the Jews did not kill Jesus, it could be argued that it does not say that Jesus was not killed on the cross. Muslims generally believe that Jesus died a natural death. To support this Surah 5:118 is quoted, where it says that Allah caused Jesus to die. Nothing is stated about natural causes in this verse, only that Allah was behind Jesus' death. Gospel believers do not have a difficult time with this concept. We believe according to the Bible that God took our iniquities and placed them on Jesus (Isaiah 53:6). We further read "Yet it pleased the Lord to bruise Him, He has put Him to grief" (Isaiah 53:10). Certainly God was watching over the sacrifice and death of the Lord Jesus Christ for the sins of the world.

WHO KILLED JESUS?

The crucifixion remains an area of stark differences between Muslims and Christians. As we have noted, the vast majority of Muslims agree that Jesus never died on the cross. There are smaller Muslim groups that do allow for Jesus' death on the cross, based on their interpretation of the Koran. Though these movements within Islam are often despised by the main stream it is interesting to note their ideas. In "The Commentator of the Koran," Maulana Muhammad Ali writes, "Some say that Jesus died on the cross for three hours, others for seven hours and so on." At the very least these comments open the door for a fresh look at the message about Jesus in the Koran.

The vast majority of Islamic scholars adhere to the idea that Jesus never died on the cross but was taken up to heaven. Still it can be argued that the Koran does not in fact deny Jesus' death on the cross, but it only denies the act was committed

35

by the Jews themselves. Most Christians would agree that it is wrong to blame the Jews for Jesus' crucifixion. While Jews were present, we know from the Biblical record that the Roman soldiers did the literal act of crucifying Jesus. In a general sense it was neither the Jews nor the Romans, but the sins of the world that crucified Jesus.

A VOICE FROM PAKISTAN

In his book, "Jesus – Contact and Conflict between Christians and Muslims," Pakistani writer Emmanuel Luther Ratiq makes a strong case in reference to how the death of Jesus could be interpreted in the Koran:

"In light of the strong evidence which scholars have provided for the crucifixion of Jesus, one cannot help concluding that if there is any evidence for any event in human history, it is for the crucifixion of Jesus Christ. This crucifixion is a proven historical fact, like other facts of history. Were there no Gospel records of it, it would still have been a fact because of the Romans, Jews and Christians, despite their differences, unanimously agree about it. There are some events which are simply recorded in the world's history, while others are recorded in religious history, but the event of the crucifixion is recorded in both. This applies to the case of the murder of Imam Hussain on the plains of Karbala, and is also valid for the crucifixion of Jesus on Golgatha. Those who say that the Quran has denied the crucifixion of Jesus, are guilty of accusing the Quran of grave ignorance of historical facts. Among Muslim scholars, there have always been those who did not want to accuse the Quran of ignorance, so they admitted freely that Jesus was crucified, died there for a short time and then was raised from the dead. This is exactly what Christians believe. Among those Muslims who believe that Jesus actually died on the Cross are:

1. Sir Syed Ahmed Khan (the founder of Aligarh Muslim University in India);
2. Maluvi Chiragh-uh-din Gamvi (the author of the famous book in Urdu entitled Minartul-Masih).

According to these Muslim scholars the Quran has not denied the event of the crucifixion of Jesus, but has only denied that the act was committed by the Jews themselves. For these Muslim scholars, to commit an act is one thing, though this does not exonerate the ones committing the act. If one denies the act, one automatically denies the guilt of those by whom it was committed. But to deny or disagree about the one who has committed the act does not necessarily deny the act itself. In the case of the crucifixion of Jesus, there were three groups on the scene besides Jesus. Those were Jesus' disciples, the Jews and the Roman authorities. The disciples did not want to see Jesus crucified. The Jews begged for his crucifixion, and the Roman rulers crucified Him."

In reference to Surah 4:157, which I quoted earlier, Mr. Ratiq writes, "The Quran does not deny the act of crucifixion, but does deny that it was the Jews who killed or crucified Jesus. Nor does it challenge the occurrence of crucifixion itself. However, Christians leave it to Muslims to find the right interpretation of verse 157 in Surah Nisaa (4), which has been commonly accepted as a negation of the crucifixion of Jesus" (Jesus – Contact and Conflict between Christians and Muslims, pg. 107-108).

THE RESURRECTION

The Koran makes it clear that Muhammad never rose from the dead (Surah 3:143-144). One Arab biographer tells of Muhammad's death on June 8th, 632 AD. According to this writer Muhammad's most beloved wife, Aisha, blamed her youth and inexperience for Muhammad's death in her lap on that very hot summer day in Arabia. She said the prophet expired "while his head was on my side between my lungs and my heart." Muhammad is buried in Medina in what is Saudi Arabia today, and millions of Muslims visit his tomb every year.

Let us highlight again some of the amazing claims concerning Jesus in the Koran:

• God moved on the virgin Mary and she conceived and had a child without ever knowing a man. Jesus had no earthly father, while Muhammad did;

• Jesus was born without sin, a virtue never attributed to Muhammad;

• Jesus healed the sick;

• God commissioned Jesus to preach the Gospel;

• One day Jesus will come back to judge the world;

• The Koran refers to Jesus 97 times, far more than Muhammad is mentioned;

• In Surah 43:63 Jesus is quoted as saying, "Follow me;"

• Jesus raised the dead back to life (Surah 5:110); and

• The Koran calls Jesus the word of God, God's Spirit, the Messiah, the sign from God, the sign for all people, the blessing from God and Mary's holy child.

We do not sweep the disagreements under the carpet, but it is news to most Christians that Jesus is even mentioned in the Koran.

THE SON OF GOD

One source of contention between Muslims and Christians is Jesus being called the "Son of God." This has not only been a stumbling block but also a source of repeated attacks and ridicule. Muslims find the idea of God engaging in a physical relationship and siring a son blasphemous. The Koran is vehemently against Jesus being called the Son of God and insists Jesus never said any such thing. I am sure that all Christians will agree that God was not involved in sexual procreation. Christians and Muslims find such a thought equally blasphemous.

In the historical context it can easily be understood why Muhammad so vehemently attacked the idea of God siring a son. Muhammad was born in 570 AD in Arabia. It was common at the time among the pagan Arab worshipers on the Arab peninsula to attribute physical births to God. Muslim writers often describe how Muhammad from an early age disliked idol worship, considering it superstition, and he never engaged in it. Muhammad passionately believed in one God, Allah, and he abhorred idol worship in any form.

WALLADULLAH OR IBN-ULLAH

In the Arab language the word for "physical son of God" is "walladullah." This word is never used in reference to Jesus Christ. Indeed, it would be blasphemous to use that word. Instead another Arab word, "ibn-ullah" is used which means "son of God" in a spiritual sense. There is a significant difference between these words, "walladullah" and "ibn-ullah." The word "ibn" is used in a metaphorical sense (in Arab literature and in the Koran) while the word "wallad" is never a metaphor, but always a direct description of a physical son.

The word "wayfarer" or "traveler" appears several times in the Koran (Surah 17:26). In Arabic it is "ibn al-sabil," which literally means "son of the road." No one would claim that the road had any physical relationship that resulted in a son. It is an illustrative expression common in many languages. We may say of a person, "he is a son of his time." The Arabic word for "Arab" could be translated "son of the desert." In the United States, you may hear the expression, "he is a son of the South." Yet no one would deduct from these expressions that "time," "the desert" or "the south" were involved in physical procreation.

Jesus is never spoken of as "walladullah," but only as "ibn-ul-lah." This distinction alone may help open a profitable dialogue between Muslims and Christians. Earlier in this chapter we looked at Jesus' virgin birth. Now let's tie things together and see the unique phrase the Bible uses to describe the birth of Jesus and how it relates to the "Son of God."

BORN OR "ONLY BEGOTTEN"

The Bible draws a distinction between the words "born" and "only begotten." Humans are born, while Jesus is the only begotten. Adam on the other hand is neither born, nor begotten; he was created. Concerning Jesus we read, "For God so loved the world that He gave His only begotten Son..." (John 3:16). The word "born" indicates an event which takes place at a specific time and has a definite beginning, while "begotten" does not imply a beginning. The term "the only begotten" is used in reference to Jesus in the sense of an un-originated relationship.

W.E. Vine's Expository Dictionary of New Testament Words gives this explanation about the phrase "the only begotten:" "The begetting is not an event in time, however remote, but a fact irrespective of time. The Christ did not become, but necessarily and eternally is, the Son. He, a Person, possesses every attribute of pure Godhood."

In other words, Jesus did not become the Son of God when He was born in Bethlehem. Instead as God is one, so Jesus had been in an eternal oneness with the Father.

MUSLIMS AND THE GOSPEL

We noted earlier that the Koran encourages people to know the Gospel. The word "Gospel" is of Greek origin. In Arabic it is "Injel." The literal meaning is "Good News." In Greek the word was rarely used before it was incorporated into the New Testament Scriptures. The reason could be that there was little use for the word due to its superlative meaning "extra-ordinary good news" or "too good to be true news."

What message could warrant a description of too good to be true news? We can be sure the Gospel is not a list of further laws or requirements from God. After all, humans have proved themselves incapable of keeping commandments, so such a list would not qualify as "good news." In my chapter "Grace not Law" we will explore the nature of the Gospel further.

I close this chapter with a word to Christians. Jesus is not a stranger to Muslims. Our views may differ, but Jesus is truly a point of contact. Talk about Jesus with the Muslims you meet. Share what Jesus has done for you, about His saving power, and you may be surprised to find friendship and openness about the person of Jesus.

41

CHAPTER FOUR

WHO IS ALLAH?

I was in Cairo, Egypt speaking to nine hundred Christian leaders. Every time I said "God," my Egyptian translator said "Allah." To some Christians from the West that would seem strange. Many don't know that Allah is simply the Arabic word for God. This name is holy and invokes great respect among Muslims. In several languages other than Arabic, the translators of the Bible also use "Allah" as the name for God. Sadly to some Christians this is unthinkable. They want nothing to do with a "Muslim" God. I have never had a Muslim object to my use of the word "God," but I have frequently heard Christians

"Hananim"

protest the word "Allah." This kind of thinking among some Christians is, damaging and very hurtful to Muslims.

"Is 'Allah' of the Koran the same as the 'God' of the Bible?"

"Dios"

When people pose this question it is important to determine what the word "same" refers to. If we refer to same characteristics the question becomes pointless. In fact "Christians" of different backgrounds do not view God's characteristics exactly the same. If the idea is to find a name for "God" that would imply sameness in our view of God, it would be quite impossible to find any name at all.

We would then be bogged down in endless discussions concerning definitions.

What if we, in an effort to be all encompassing, would include Hollywood and its definitions of God? I think we can agree that we would never find a suitable name for the Almighty. After all, what Christian theologians would agree that actors like Jim Carrey, Morgan Freeman or George Burns provide theologically accurate depictions of God.

Christians are often heard declaring that the God of the Bible is not the God of the Muslims. This is a strange logic for we could just as well say the God of many Christians is not the God of the Bible.

The only fruitful question must be if the word "Allah" means the same in Arabic as the word "God" does in English. It is crucial that we understand this question so let's look deeper into this.

Both the Bible and the Koran are clear God is not the God of one group, but of all people. The Bible states, "The earth is the LORD's, and all its fullness, the world and those who dwell therein" (Psalm 24:1), and "He is a God of all flesh" (Jeremiah 32:27). There are numerous references in the Koran, which make it clear that Muslims believe the God of Christians and Jews is the Almighty. Before we look at experience, culture and the Bible itself concerning this matter, one thing needs to be understood: Muslims consider Allah to be the Supreme, Almighty, in the same way as Christians speak of God as Almighty.

GOD IN EVERY LANGUAGE

Every language has a name for God. I recently visited western Indonesia and asked one of the tribal groups what their name for the Almighty was. They replied, "Mansreen." So when their translation of the Bible quotes from John 3:16 it says, "Mansreen so loved the world." Does that sound strange?

In Finland the Finnish name for God is "Jumala." The Finnish Bible reads Genesis 1:1, "In the beginning, 'Jumala' created heaven and earth." The Mandarin Chinese name for God is "Shang Ti." The Russian name is "Bog." In Korean the Supreme Being is called "Hananim." Does it seem foreign for you to pray to Hananim in the name of Jesus?

In German, God is called "Gott," in French, "Dieu," in Spanish, "Dios" and in English, "God." Every language and culture has its own name for the Supreme Being. *The problem arises when one language group considers its name for God more holy than the name for God in another language.*

ELAH, ELOH & ALLAH

"Eloh"

The Hebrew name for God is "Eloh" and in Aramaic, the language Jesus spoke, it is "Elah." This bears no resemblance to our English word "God" or any of the other languages I cited. Hebrew, Aramaic and Arabic are closely related languages. At times the letters "A" or "E" become "I" when pronouncing a Hebrew or Aramaic word in Arabic. Abraham becomes Ibrahim. When you put the words "Elah" (Aramaic) and "Allah" (Arabic) side by side, you see how close they are. The word, "Elah," would become "Ilah" in Arabic. When you attach the definitive form "Al" it becomes "Al-Ilah," (The God), which then becomes "Allah." The similarity is obvious. Allah is simply the Arabic name for Almighty God.

IS "GOD" THE RIGHT NAME FOR GOD?

When Christians say that Allah is not a correct name for God, this is very offensive to our Muslim friends. Sometimes Christians say, "We don't believe in Allah; we believe in God." One

"Shang Ti"

might logically ask, "Where does the word "God" come from?" After all, "God" is not at all similar to the Biblical Hebrew name "Eloh." In fact, God is the Germanic name for the Supreme Being, a name that in its origin has nothing to do with Christianity. "God" was the word for the Supreme Creator used by the people of central and northern Europe thousands of years ago. English, German, Swedish, Norwegian and Danish are all Germanic languages. The English word "God," becomes "Gott" in German, "Gud" in Swedish and so on. It is easy to see the linguistic relationship.

NOT A TRIBAL GOD

Some Christians have ignorantly claimed that Allah is a tribal Arabic "god." When preachers claim that Muhammed elevated his tribal god above the other desert tribes, they are at best showing ignorance and at worst re-writing history. While it is true that before Muhammad preached about Allah, the tribes living in the Arabian Desert believed and worshiped various gods including the moon god, this has nothing to do with the use of the word "Allah." Long before Muhammad's preaching, Allah was the Arabic name for God, the Supreme Almighty.

When so called "authorities" claim that Allah is the "moon God," they are perpetuating a myth. No Muslim has ever associated Allah with any deity other than the One spoken of by Abraham, Moses, David and a host of other prophets. Muhammad was very clear in his preaching of one God, the Creator of all.

If we were to trace the original meaning of the Hebrew "Eloh" and the Arabic "Ilah," we would discover the same root meanings, "The Exalted One." Ask any Muslim and you will discover that Allah refers to the Supreme Almighty God.

MISREPRESENTATIONS OF GOD

Christians may argue that they do not want to use the word

Allah because they disagree with the Islamic understanding of God. We need to remember that there are many disagreements about God, also among Christians.

One horrifying example is the Nazi soldiers during the second world-war, who had an inscription on their belt buckle, "Gott mit uns," meaning "God with us." The very soldiers who implemented the Holocaust confessed faith in God on their belt buckles. Do you agree with their view on God? Of course not! That does not mean, however, that we should change the German word for God. People can misrepresent God in any language or religion. Look in any bookstore and you will find literature about God where the content is not even remotely describing the God we know through the Bible. Hollywood has already been mentioned as a frequent distorter of God. Yet we do not suggest that we should erase the word "God" from the English language because someone misrepresents God or attaches false attributes to God.

DISASTERS, TSUNAMIS AND STROKE

I frequently come across misrepresentations of God. When the Tsunami hit Southeast Asia in December, 2004, one Christian preacher claimed this was God's judgment on prostitution in Thailand. I, for one, have a diametrically opposite view of God. The God I know poured all of His wrath over human sin upon Jesus at the cross (Isaiah 53:4-6). He did not send a Tsunami to kill people who in many cases had never had a single opportunity to hear the Gospel. The only judgment we will have to face is concerning what we do with Jesus (Romans 2:16). [See Chapter 5, "Grace not Law."]

Another Christian preacher claimed that the stroke suffered by Israeli Prime Minister Ariel Sharon in early 2006 was God's judgment. Still another minister suggested that hurricane

Katrina that hit New Orleans in the fall of 2005 was God's judgment over U.S. President Bush's Middle East policies. According to this preacher President Bush's supposed sin was to have encouraged Israel to pull out of Gaza. These are false caricatures of God. Why would God single out New Orleans, and particularly why would this supposed judgment fall on people, who were too poor to own a car which would have helped them flee before the impending catastrophe? I differ completely with these strange views of God. Yet, these misguided views of God do not cause me to want to change the word "God." Instead I am inspired to preach a proper Gospel-based view of God. I want to show the world that God already poured His judgment for our sins on Jesus.

The argument that Muslims have a different view of God does not warrant discrediting the name of Allah. When Christians attack the use of the word Allah they cause unnecessary confrontation and often irreparable hurt. Of course Christians and Muslims have disagreement about certain things concerning God's character, but we must not be ignorant and cast aside an entire language group's expression for their Creator, Almighty God.

PAUL AND THE GREEKS

Each culture has its own name for the Supreme Being. In the Greek culture, that name was Zeus. When Paul said, "For in Him we live and move and have our being, as also some of your own poets have said, 'For we are also His offspring'" (Acts 17:28), he was quoting poems that had been written in honor of Zeus (see Chapter 7, "Respect Without Compromise"). Notice Paul does not try to convince the Athenians that they should adapt a new "Christian" name for God; he used the local name.

Among all people you find a name for the Creator God, the Sky God, the Great God, the Almighty. It is an ultimate insult to Muslims when Christians say that Allah is not God. When I visit Indonesia, I read from the English Bible and my translator reads from the Indonesian Bible. Every time the word "God" appears in my English Bible my translator says "Allah." The same is true in a host of other countries. Christians in the Western world must not allow ignorance and bigotry to dominate our thinking, but rather we must follow the approach of Jesus and the apostle Paul.

KOREA VS. JAPAN

I mentioned earlier that the Korean name for God is Hananim. The Gospel of Jesus Christ has had great success in Korea. Some have suggested one of the reasons is that the first Gospel preachers who came to Korea did not try to import a western or "Christian" name for God; they simply took the name for the Supreme Being that the Koreans already had in their language. In other countries like Japan, Christian missionaries thought it necessary to import a foreign name for God or create a new name for God. In the local culture this became known as the "Christian God." In countries where a "Christian" name for God was taught, the Gospel has had limited success.

ALLAH ON THE DAY OF PENTECOST

The Day of Pentecost is very important in the Christian calendar. It was on this day the Holy Spirit became readily available to all believers. The Book of Acts gives a full description of this remarkable day, and all indications are that some of the people present were praising Allah. We read in Acts 2:11, "Cretans and Arabs - we hear them speaking in our own tongues the wonderful works of God." If Arabs were declaring the wonderful works of God in their own tongue, what word were they using? Obviously they used the word "Allah," their name for the Supreme Being.

There is only one God. He is the God of all people, the God of the universe and the Lord of all the earth. He is not a Muslim God, a Christian God, a Buddhist God, a Hindu God, or some other Gods. There is one God, the God of the entire world. Paul never said, "I come to you to preach about the Christian God." No, he declared God, the Creator of heaven and earth, and how the Almighty had revealed Himself through Jesus.

God loves the whole world. True Jesus followers do not blaspheme or disrespect other religions. Why argue about things that the apostle Paul never debated? Accept that God has put eternity in every person's heart, and that every language has its own name for the Supreme Being.

WHAT ABOUT THE "THREE-IN-ONE"?

One of the major objections Muslims will raise is about the Trinity. Many Muslims are aware that the word "Trinity" is not in the Bible and they wonder why Christians believe such a seemingly illogical doctrine. "Do Christians worship three gods?" is a question posed. The answer is emphatically and unequivocally NO! GOD IS ONE, REVEALED IN THREE PERSONS.

It has already been noted in a previous chapter that the term "Son of God" does not imply a biological Father and Son relationship. Now, let's look at God revealed in three persons: Father, Son and Holy Spirit, which the Bible clearly teaches. Does this revelation in three persons take away from the fact that GOD IS ONE, or does it merely reveal more of God's true nature?

WHY THE FATHER?

Most religions agree that God is Almighty, that He is the High and Holy One. It is Jesus, who reveals the Eternal One as our Father. The Father concept was distasteful to the Pharisees who listened to Jesus' sermons. They saw God only as a Law-giver and a Judge.

The apostle Paul uses the Greek word, "Abba," to describe God. Abba simply means "daddy." To many, including Christians, this seems almost blasphemous and too familiar. How can the Almighty be called "Dad?" Yet without God revealed as a Father how can we know Him? Presenting God as a Father attracted the multitudes to Jesus' teaching. He said things about God that they had never heard before. God was no longer out of touch, far away in space, but close, touchable and compassionate.

WHY THE SON?

A careful reader of the Bible will notice Jesus is not described as "born" of God, but "begotten" of God. He is "the only begotten" from the Father. Had Jesus been born of God, then it would imply physical relationship, while the term "begotten" speaks only of a spiritual communion (see chapter 3).

Why was it necessary that God had to be revealed as "The Son?" This again goes back to our human inability. We could not and cannot reach God by our own initiative – God had to come to us.

Our sinfulness made it *necessary* for God to come to earth as the Son. Our sins had made it impossible for us to reach God; instead God had to reach us.

God's unconditional love for all people makes Jesus' coming as the Son of God *understandable*. It is makes perfect sense that a loving God would want relationship with His created beings, especially as those created beings [us] were made for fellowship with our Maker.

Both the Koran and the Bible agree that God can do whatever He desires, no matter how strange or inexplicable it is to humans. God's ability to do anything, even that which seems illogical to the human mind makes Jesus' coming as the Son of God *believable*.

WHY THE HOLY SPIRIT?

Already at the creation of the world "the Spirit of God moved" upon the waters. The Holy Spirit empowered Jesus as both the Bible and the Koran testify. One such reference is in Surah 5:110, "Then will Allah say: 'O Jesus the son of Mary...I strengthened thee with the holy spirit." Who is the Holy Spirit God and why does God have to be revealed in the person of the Holy Spirit?

Jesus prophesied that when He would return to heaven, the Holy Spirit would be our Comforter "with us" and "in us," not only for a season but "forever" (John 14:16). This means the term "Comforter" or "the Holy Spirit" cannot refer to a human, not even a prophet, because no human can be "with" and "in" every believer "forever." It cannot be a reference to Elijah, Muhammad, Moses or any other limited human.

It is necessary for God to be revealed in the person of The Holy Spirit, in order that every believer will have an inward witness of the reality of God. This is a wonderful love. God doesn't merely want to be an idea, a concept or a distant Almighty. He wants to live in people. In fact, it is only by God's presence in people that we can truly be righteous. His indwelling presence empowers us to do what we could never do in our own ability.

The Holy Spirit is the One who works inside those who believe on Jesus, reminding us of what Jesus has done for us by His death and resurrection. This is extremely helpful because in practical day-by-day living it is easy to look at negative circumstances instead of looking at what Jesus has done. When

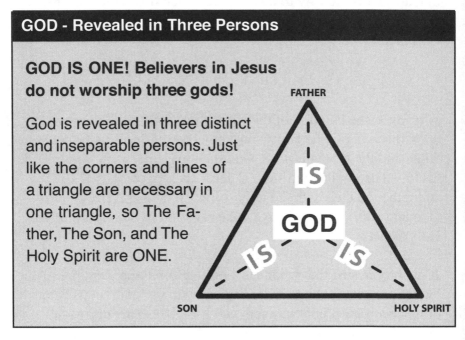

GOD - Revealed in Three Persons

GOD IS ONE! Believers in Jesus do not worship three gods!

God is revealed in three distinct and inseparable persons. Just like the corners and lines of a triangle are necessary in one triangle, so The Father, The Son, and The Holy Spirit are ONE.

FATHER

IS

GOD

IS   IS

SON   HOLY SPIRIT

we look at our own inadequacies we are easily discouraged, but when the Holy Spirit helps us focus our attention on Jesus and what He has done for us, we are strengthened.

GOD TRANSCENDS LOGIC

Father, Son and Holy Spirit are not three persons in the way we look at three distinct humans. Like H_2O is revealed in three distinct forms; ice, liquid water and vapor, so God is also revealed. I will be the first to acknowledge that this transcends human logic. Isn't that the way God often does things? His logic is higher than ours. This is why faith is needed. Let's not mock or ridicule the inexplicable.

There are many things Muslims and Christians accept by faith, without being able to logically explain it. For example Muslims believe that Muhammad was taken to heaven in an instant to negotiate with Allah concerning the frequency of prayers required by Muslims. Later that day Muhammad was back on earth telling his followers about the experience. Such accounts transcend human logic.

The idea of God revealed in three persons cannot fully be explained from the point of view of the human mind. Yet, viewed from *the position of human need* the Triune God is easily understood. People need God to be more than a Judge; we need a Father, but to know God as a Father someone had to come to earth to reveal Him. No human qualified, as all were sinners, even the prophets, so God had to be revealed as the Son. The Bible calls it the "mystery of godliness." Jesus said, "No one has seen God at any time. The only begotten God, who is in the bosom of the Father, He has declared Him" (John 1:18). It was necessary for God, the Son, to come in order that people would know God is love, full of compassion to heal, forgive, and restore. However, God must not be revealed only to one select group of people in one period of history. We need to know God individually each day. The Holy Spirit indwells those who believe in Jesus, and this satisfies the universal human longing for God.

NO CONTRADICTION

For 33 years Jesus lived in a limited human body, especially prepared for Him. During His 33 years on earth, Jesus made seemingly contradictory statements like "My Father and I are one," and "My Father is greater than I." How could both these sayings be true?

On the one hand the limitations of Jesus' earthly body made the Father "greater" for those 33 years. While on earth Jesus laid aside the independent use of divine power. Notice, I didn't say He laid aside His divine power or attributes, only the independent use of them. Jesus lived for 33 years in complete dependency on His Father, and He only exercised divine power at the direction of His Father. This self-imposed human limitation, which ended by Jesus' resurrection from the dead, makes the statement "My Father is greater than I" perfectly understandable, and it does not negate Jesus' oneness with His Father.

Look at the triangle, which is an illustrative way to show God revealed in the three persons. Though no illustration is perfect, this depiction gives a glimpse of the awesomeness of God.

Who is Allah? First, let's settle once and for all that "Allah" is the Arabic name for God, and that this name is holy to Muslims. Christians and Muslims differ in some of the ways we view God, but Christians also differ on this subject. Still, both groups believe in ONE GOD. Regardless of different views of God, all sensible people will agree that each language has its own name for God. In Arabic that name for God is Allah.

CHAPTER FIVE

GRACE NOT LAW

The grace of Jesus is without comparison in any philosophy or religion. Grace is the <u>undeserved</u>, <u>unearned</u>, <u>unmerited</u> favor of God available to each person because of Jesus. God's blessings are available, not on the basis of our good works, but because of what Jesus has done.

Through Adam the whole world became sinners. This is evident in Adam's descendants, and it is evident today. Though we were not present in the Garden of Eden when Adam sinned, his sin was passed on to every generation – including you and me. Each human was born in sin (Romans 3:10, 23). We did not work for our sinfulness; it happened to us because of Adam's disobedience. Herein lies a key to understand how we are made righteous. Just as we were made sinners by one man's (Adam's) disobedience, we are made righteous by another man's obedience. That one man is Jesus, who took our sins on Himself. *God punished Jesus for every sin we would ever commit.* Jesus became our substitute, taking our place.

This demonstrates God's unconditional love for us. He has not only taken our sins; He has offered us something for FREE – His righteousness. This is not about what we should do to get to God, but what God has freely done for us.

Jesus was God revealed in human flesh, which explains why He was perfect and without sin. Both the Bible and the Koran agree about Jesus' sinlessness. One sinner could not die for another sinner anymore than one murderer can die on behalf of another murderer. Jesus, the perfect one, fulfilled every requirement of God's law.

At the moment of His death on the cross Jesus cried out; "It is fulfilled" (Matthew 5:17-18). What was "fulfilled?" The answer is that the requirements of total obedience to the commandments of God had been fulfilled. Jesus did what no one had ever done; He lived the perfect sinless life. The Bible as well as the Koran also acknowledge Jesus' sinlessness (Surah 3:35).

Simply put, Jesus' death on the cross solves the human problem of sin.

Since the sins of the world have been put away once and for all by Jesus' sacrifice, those sins are no longer a problem that separate man from God. Jesus removed the obstacle of sin and now the only potential obstacle to peace with God is if a person rejects the Good News message of what Jesus has done. Jesus said, "He who believes is saved, he who does not believe is condemned." Now because of what Jesus did the whole world, every culture, every language, every group of people are invited to receive God's righteousness as a free gift.

We benefit from this free gift only when we receive it. Ponder what this "free gift" really is. *It is Christ's perfect righteousness given to us.* Without it we can never please God because of the inadequacy of our own righteousness. Our attempt at being righteous is filthy and unacceptable to God. No matter how many sacrifices and prayers we offer our holiness will never measure up to God's holiness.

The miracle of Jesus' death on the cross is that He put away our sins by one sacrifice. By believing and receiving this, we open the door for God to work inside of us. Jesus imparts His righteousness and life to us when we ask Him in prayer. To be a true follower of Jesus is simply to allow His life to be lived in us. We yield to His love, faith and righteousness in us.

RULES OR PHILOSOPHY

Grace is a difficult topic for all religions. Most adhere to one of two other ways of "salvation:" rules or philosophy, or a combination of both. Both rules and philosophy have their place. We need rules in traffic and laws in society. Philosophy helps people evaluate the world.

Philosophy has to do with a metaphysical approach to God: thinking, meditating, and studying until spiritual enlightenment comes. One popular philosophical teaching advocates that everything can be reduced to the energy of brain waves. Through meditation and concentration, one taps into an energy field that could be described as "god." Several major world religions endeavor to find God through a similar philosophical pursuit.

Trying to find God by the adherence to strict codes of moral and ceremonial rules is prevalent. If you were to ask a Pharisee within the religion of Judaism, "How can I find God?" the response would be, "Keep the rules." Has anyone been able to keep all the commandments of God? Some would say "Yes;" others might honestly respond, "Not completely." The truth is none of us are capable of living up to all the commandments. The Bible is clear in describing the human inability to live up to God's standards.

In the Koran you find many descriptions of how the Jewish people had failed to follow God's commandments. This was a major topic of Muhammad's preaching. Still Muhammad and all the prophets in the Koran also failed, which is why Allah commanded Muhammad in the Koran to "ask forgiveness for thy sin and for believing men." (Surah 47:19). The witness is clear that rules cannot make us righteous.

In the Bible the main proponents of philosophical religion were the Greeks. The apostle Paul faced this dilemma of rules and philosophy. He said, "The Jews (people of rules and morality) request a sign, and Greeks (people of philosophy) seek after wisdom" (1 Corinthians 1:22). When we preach Jesus Christ and what He has done on the cross this becomes a stumbling block to the people of rules (Jews) and foolishness to the people of philosophy (Greeks).

When our focus is to keep rules in order to please God the message of Christ's righteousness as a free gift seems *too easy*. It seems *too good to be true* that peace with God can be enjoyed by only believing in what Jesus has done. On the other hand, if your pursuit has been philosophy, which tends to be complicated to the point that the adherents of philosophy admit they do not fully understand it, the Gospel also appears *too simple*. The philosopher may say, "It can't be that simple." The apostle Paul writes, "For the message of the cross is foolishness to those who are perishing, but to us who are being saved it is the power of God" (1 Corinthians 1:18).

Now, look with me again at the simplicity of the Gospel story. What is this powerful "message of the cross?"

GOD REVEALED IN JESUS

The Gospel is that God, who is holy, just and righteous, loves the world. The world's dilemma was its inability to reach God. Since every person was contaminated by sin, we were incapable of reaching the high and holy Almighty. The only solution

60

was that God Himself would become a human; the Almighty would take upon Himself human flesh, and walk among us to show us what God is like. Jesus' loving treatment of sinners and of sick, hurting, and hopeless people tells us how God views humanity.

Jesus explained, "No one has seen God at any time. The only begotten Son, who is in the bosom of the Father, He has declared Him" (John 1:18). Jesus is clear. He is the only one qualified to show us who God really is. Centuries and millennia of tradition and religion in many layers had removed people's knowledge of who God really is. Jesus came to restore a proper view of God.

The wonder does not end there. Earlier I mentioned the word "substitute." What does it mean? Jesus took the judgment of our sin, our sicknesses, our pain and our punishment. He suffered the ultimate consequence of sin, which is death, not for Himself, but for us. Jesus took our place of death. As great as this is, there is more. Jesus conquered death and rose again. Because Jesus now lives, He is able to save everyone who comes to God through Him.

IS THIS TOO SIMPLE?

Compared with complicated philosophy, this story indeed seems too simple. This is why some called the apostle Paul a "babbler." Who could believe such an uncomplicated message? People who pursue God through philosophy tend to want something deep and inexplicable. The story of the Gospel has such a simple beauty that it offends the mind which craves complicated answers.

How is such a message even believable? God says that He Himself will bear witness inside each person who becomes a child of God. If it weren't for this direct involvement of God in the Gospel it simply would be an "all too incredible story." God promises that those who receive the message of the Gospel will receive the wisdom and the power of Jesus Christ. Jesus Himself will impart life and righteousness to the one who calls upon Him.

The Gospel stands in contrast to all religion. *We do not come to God by what we can do, but by what Jesus has already done.* All we have to do is believe and receive. We do not have to cleanse ourselves, purify ourselves or make ourselves worthy. In fact, we are incapable of doing any of those things adequately. Instead, we only and solely trust in what Jesus has done. He alone is our hope, our salvation and our righteousness.

MUSLIMS SACRIFICE A LAMB

When people first hear this message you can almost see them gasp, because it is so different. When I share the Gospel with my Muslim friends, I often remind them that tradition within Islamic culture testifies of the amazing sacrifice Jesus made. Devout Muslims sacrifice a lamb annually in commemoration of the great prophet Abraham. The Muslim holiday "Idul Adha" comes at the end of the Islamic year, and is known as a time of sacrifice. Though most families offer a lamb or a goat, wealthier families may sacrifice a cow.

When Abraham's son was placed on the altar of sacrifice, he should have died, but God provided a lamb to take his place. I never argue about whether it was Isaac or Ishmael on the altar, because on this point Muslims and Christians differ. Muslims believe it was Ishmael, while Christians believe it was Isaac. My objective is to get to the main point of the Gospel message, which is what Jesus has done for us.

Abraham's son should have died. He represents us because we should die because of our sin. God in His great love told Abraham not to kill his son. Instead, God provided a lamb to take the place of Abraham's son. John the Baptist, who is the prophet Yehya in the Koran, pointed to Jesus and said, "Behold! The Lamb of God who takes away the sin of the world!" (John 1:29) The lamb became the substitute for Abraham's son just like Jesus became our substitute. We should have been killed and judged for our sins but God provided the Lamb of God to take our place.

THE WORLD'S SINS ARE PUT AWAY

When we speak of God's grace, we focus on the cross and resurrection of Jesus. We read, "...all things are of God, who has reconciled us to Himself through Jesus Christ." Most Christians have no difficulty in embracing this truth. Certainly Christians believe they have been reconciled to God by Jesus' death on the cross.

The apostle Paul continues, "...God was in Christ reconciling the world to Himself, not imputing their trespasses to them, and has committed to us the word of reconciliation" (2 Corinthians 5:18-19).

This is an astounding statement. Christ's death not only includes those who believe on Him; but the world – the whole wide world – was reconciled to God. *God has put away the sins of the world through what Jesus did.* That is why John the Baptist said that Jesus "takes away" the sins of the world. This prophecy of removing the world's sins has been fulfilled. You may ask "when did it happen?" It happened at the cross.

The apostle John says that Jesus is, "the propitiation for our sins, and not for ours only but also for the whole world" (1 John 2:2).

This is a recurring theme throughout the New Testament. What God did in Jesus, He did for the world. Jesus is "the Savior of all men, especially of those who believe" (1 Timothy 4:10). There is only one Savior for all people: the Lord Jesus Christ! God's blessings in Jesus are available equally to all, but only those who believe in Him enjoy the blessings.

ARE ALL SAVED?

Though Jesus Christ reconciled every person to God by His death, this does not mean that every human is saved. If that were the case there would be no need to share the Good News of God's love in Christ to every person. If eternal life and peace with God were automatic there would be no urgency to share this message.

In order to be saved we must receive Jesus' life into us as we read in Romans 5:10: "For if when we were enemies we were reconciled to God through the death of His Son, much more, having been reconciled, we shall be saved by His life."

The two parts are obvious. First, our sins have been put away. This is already done, an accomplished fact, whether we believe it or not. Secondly, when we receive Jesus' life in us we are saved. The moment we believe, His life comes into us.

GOD'S FAVOR TO EVERYONE

Look again at what Paul said about God reconciling the world to Himself:

"It was God [personally present] in Christ, reconciling and restoring the world to favor with Himself, not counting up and holding against [men] their trespasses [but canceling them], and committing to us the message of reconciliation (of the restoration to favor)." 2 Corinthians 5:19 AMP

1. God does not count or hold the world's sins against people. This sounds blasphemous to some, but when we understand the Gospel, we see that Jesus took away the sins of the world. His redemptive work is without limits. *The crucial question now is whether or not a person has received Jesus.* He who has Jesus has eternal life. The Holy Spirit convicts people concerning "not believing in Jesus" (John 16:8-11). When we tell people what Jesus has done, we are co-operating with the Holy Spirit. When the apostles preached this the conviction became so great that people cried out, "What shall we do to be saved?" When we share God's love with Muslims, Christians or people of any religion, we tell them what Jesus has done and how they can receive God's righteousness made available through Jesus Christ.

2. The world's sins have been cancelled by Jesus. When an event is cancelled, it is not happening anymore.

3. God has restored the world to favor. People no longer need to come to God with fear and trepidation because God is already favorably inclined to the world. How? Not by the good things that we produce, but by the good Jesus has done.

4. We are ministers of reconciliation. Our job is to tell the world what Jesus has done. Since God is no longer unreconciled toward people, so much more reason for us to, "be reconciled to God" (2 Corinthians 5:20). Let's put it in different words. If God is not angry with us, let's make sure we are not angry toward God. Why would we be? He is the one who loves us. All that

is left for people is to receive Jesus. His death on the cross reconciled us to God and when we receive His life we are saved (Romans 5:10).

How do we become righteous? Is it by what we do? Certainly not! We become righteous by what Jesus has done. As we reciprocate and respond to God's love, we are saved. Once we are saved we receive power to live holy and dedicated lives in service to God (Romans 5:19-21).

GOD'S NOT ANGRY

God's anger over sin is recorded numerous times in the Bible as well as the Koran. God was so angry He sent a flood in the day of Noah to wipe out the human race. On another occasion, God sent fire over two cities (Sodom and Gomorrah) because of their sin.

Today the Good News is that God is not angry. God's wrath over sin was poured on Jesus. We read, "And the LORD has laid on Him the iniquity of us all" (Isaiah 53:6). The judgment (punishment) we should have received was put on Jesus.

Isaiah continues, "The chastisement (judgment) for our peace was upon Him." We should have been chastised, beaten and punished with eternal death. Instead, Jesus took our punishment so that we should receive peace. This is good news. God is smiling. This is the day of grace. When the free gift of Jesus' righteousness is offered, all we can do is respond with a "No," or a "Yes."

HAS GOD CHANGED?

When we speak of God's grace, some argue that we claim God has changed from the Old Testament to the New Testament.

Not at all. God has always hated sin. When Jesus hung on the cross God finally did what He always wanted to do to sin. God beat up on sin when He poured His wrath upon Jesus. The anger of God that should have fallen on us fell on Jesus.

This is not a matter of God being angry and judgmental in the Old Testament and kind and loving in the New Testament. God was always a kind, loving and merciful God. He provided a system of sacrifices by which people could have their sins covered in the Old Testament. God never takes pleasure in judgment on anyone. He does not even take pleasure in the death of the wicked. After God's anger over human sin had fallen upon Jesus on the cross, God could show His true nature of love and mercy to the world. Now, sin does not need to be punished anymore since it has already been judged. The only future punishment is for those who do not receive the free gift of Jesus' righteousness. The apostle Paul calls this "judgment to come" (Acts 24:26).

This fantastic message of God's love has been given to us in order that we would pass it on to others. We are to tell people, "Be reconciled to God" because God is reconciled to you.

The apostle Paul used this approach. When he preached in Athens, he referred to an altar with the inscription, "To the Unknown God." He didn't tell the people of Athens that their God was the wrong God nor that they needed a Christian God. He recognized that the Athenians were already aware of the Supreme Being. They had already tried to worship the Almighty the best they knew how. Paul's job was not to ridicule or put down what they were already trying to do with all sincerity, but to bring revelation about this God.

LESS RELIGION, MORE JESUS

We need not act as representatives of Christianity. Much good has been done in the name of Christianity, but regrettably also much evil. We have made so much of the word "Christianity," yet Jesus never used that word. The word "Christian" only appears twice in the entire Bible. Often words like "grace," "faith," "righteousness" and "love" which are found many times throughout the Bible, take a backseat to the word "Christian." Let's put less on the religion of Christianity and more on the person of Jesus.

Sadly, many Christians do not know Jesus in a personal relationship. I often tell my Muslim friends "Do not think I am only sharing Jesus with you. I share Jesus just as much with Christians and people of other religions. We all need Jesus."

The apostle Paul put it this way, "But what does it say? 'The word is near you, in your mouth and in your heart' [that is, the word of faith which we preach]: that if you confess with your mouth the Lord Jesus and believe in your heart that God has raised Him from the dead, you will be saved. For with the heart one believes unto righteousness, and with the mouth confession is made unto salvation" (Romans 10:8-10).

Now receive God's grace.

1. Believe in your heart that God raised Jesus from the dead. Ask God to help you believe, because when you ask, Jesus promised you would receive.

2. Confess that Jesus is your Lord.

That's all you need. Now lift up your voice and thank God for His gift of salvation. It's yours because of Jesus.

CHAPTER SIX

THE MIRACLE FACTOR

There are several ways a religion increases its membership. Biological growth is one. Parents teach religion to their children; they teach their grandchildren, and so on. Wars have affected people's religion. You conquer a geographical territory, and teach - or worse enforce - your religion upon those you have subjugated. Sadly this form of "conversion" has been done by all religions.

Jesus has a different approach. His method is for individuals, one by one, to be born again. Jesus said, "Unless one is born again, he cannot see the kingdom of God" (John 3:3). To be born again is to receive new life, a new nature, from Jesus. That's the greatest miracle of all. No amount of human effort can make a person born again. It is God who does this work in each person individually.

When someone calls on Jesus, that person will never be ashamed. Jesus imparts His faith and His righteousness in those who call upon Him. The Holy Spirit comes to reside in that person and gives witness inside of the new life, which has come. We do not have to convince people of the reality of Jesus once they have the inward witness of Jesus Himself. *Jesus makes Himself known inside of people.* That is why I encourage Christians, Muslims, Hindus, Buddhists, Jews or atheists, to call on Jesus and let His life come inside of them. The miracle of being born again cuts through all arguments and debate. It becomes a personal witness of the reality of Jesus.

MUSLIM BOY HEALED

There are other miracles in addition to being born again, most commonly they are physical healings. I have witnessed thousands of healings among all kinds of people, including many Muslims. With my own eyes I have seen the lame, blind, deaf and cancer patients from virtually all non-Christian religions receive healing through Jesus. Many stories come to mind, but let me tell the first healing of a Muslim that I can recall.

This happened in 1980 during a nine-day Gospel Festival in East Africa. On the last day of the Festival, a woman dressed in black with only her face showing came to the platform with her thirteen-year-old boy. She told an amazing story. "First, I did not want to come to this meeting. I associated it with the religion of Christianity and thought it had nothing to do with me. Then I heard that miracles of healing happened to people, so I thought I would bring my boy. Ever since he was born he has suffered from epileptic seizures. We have visited many doctors but there was no cure. In fact, my son has never gone for more than two days without a seizure. Recently, it has been every night. My husband and I take turns at his bedside. Nine nights ago we stood way in the back where no one could see us and listened to your words about God's love in Jesus. We listened to the prayers and went home that night. Amazingly, the whole night went by without any seizure. We came back eight nights ago, seven nights ago and so on; every night we went home and now nine nights have passed without any seizure. This has never happened before. We know that Jesus has done a wonder."

MUHAMMAD IN KARACHI

A middle-aged engineer named Muhammad was crying on
our platform in Karachi, Pakistan. When I asked him why he
was sad, he responded, "I am not sad; I am happy. Look at my
four-year-old girl. She was born blind. When you prayed in
the name of Jesus tonight, she has received her sight."

Jesus said that wherever we go and preach His Gospel, He
would confirm it with miracles. Jesus' disciples in the first
century after Christ experienced this, and we still see it today.
We read, "They went out and preached everywhere, the Lord
working with them and confirming the word through the accompanying signs" (Mark 16:20).

It is Jesus' plan that He would supernaturally confirm His
Gospel. Without miracles all we have are conflicting theories
and philosophies. I have found that it is just as easy to see
God's miraculous love touch Muslims, as it is for Christians
or people of any other religion to receive from God. God is
not a discriminator. Some Christians have difficulty with this.
They protest when God heals Muslims in our Festivals thinking that they should be first in line for any divine blessing. I
remind people there is not a single record of Jesus ever healing
a Christian. There were no Christians two thousand years ago.
Jesus simply healed and touched people, and He is the same
today.

REAL MIRACLES VERIFIED

We do not try to convince our Muslim friends that Jesus does
miracles today. Let each person watch and see for themselves.
When journalists ask me if the miracles are real, I simply ask
them to interview the people who have been healed. Talk
to the family members, doctors, and most of all, the patients

themselves. A genuine miracle will stand up to a test. The Gospel without miracles is just words and theories. We know from the records of the New Testament that many believed when they saw the miracles of Jesus. Others still refused to believe in the face of the miraculous happenings around them. It is the same today. Some will not believe, no matter what is being said or seen, but many will come to Jesus when they see proof that He is alive today.

JESUS - NOT MAGIC

Many religions believe that supernatural phenomena are possible through special holy persons or at certain holy places. The whole concept of miracles is shrouded in mystery and magic. People give money and recite incantations to appease God. This has nothing to do with the miracles of Jesus.

How do we know a miracle comes from Jesus? First of all we know because no human takes credit for it. Jesus-believers experience miracles, not because of their own power or holiness, but by simple faith in Jesus. When we preach what Jesus has done, God comes on the scene to confirm the words that have been spoken by granting miracles.

God's genuine miracles do not bring fear and anxiety upon the recipients. Rather, His miracles are accompanied by a sense of great love and peace. Miracles are simple expressions of God's love for people.

I am writing this chapter while traveling in Indonesia. This week I have been preaching to a capacity crowd in a stadium every night. Many people of all ages have testified of having received a miracle from Jesus. A young boy named Muhammad was completely deaf and had his hearing restored. An older Muslim man had suffered a debilitating stroke, losing both his speech and ability to walk. His family brought him to the stadium and now he is back to normal. He told his family that when the multitude lifted their hands in praise to Jesus, he saw a light enter his body and he knew this was Jesus' healing power.

Miracles happen when the Good News of God's love revealed through Jesus is preached. We should not be surprised when God does this; it is His nature.

CHAPTER SEVEN

RESPECT WITHOUT COMPROMISE

Jesus is our example of showing respect toward others. We have already noted it was common two thousand years ago for Samaritans to show disdain toward Jews, and Jews to reciprocate toward the Samaritans. Jesus demonstrated equal respect for both groups.

The apostle Paul showed respect for the people of Athens who worshiped various gods. He did not agree with them, but he respected them. It is possible to respect people without agreeing with their beliefs.

The Bible sets a pattern for us to build bridges between people by highlighting the things we do agree on. Could this be why the apostle Paul quotes two Greek poets, Epiminedes and Cleothos of Assos? "'For in Him we live and move and have our being,' as also some of your own poets have said, 'For we are also His offspring'" (Acts 17:28).

Who were these two poets? Epiminedes was from Crete and around 620 BC he wrote, "The creation dug out a grave for you, O holy and high (Zeus). Liars, evil beasts and lazy gluttons are they. Because you did not die, you live eternally and remain, in you we live, move and have our being." The quote "for we are also His offspring," is from a third century B.C. writing by Cleothos of Assos.

Some today may have accused the apostle of compromising by quoting non-Christian sources. On the contrary, Paul was building bridges of understanding and mutual friendship. Note that though Epiminedes had written his poem in honor of Zeus, Paul saw no need to say anything derogatory concerning the word Zeus. This was the Greek word for God, just like every language has its own word for the Almighty (see chapter 4: Who is Allah?). This doesn't mean the apostle Paul agreed with Greek religion. It simply shows that it is possible to respect and value other people's beliefs without compromising our own.

RESPECT FOR ABRAHAM

Muslims and Christians share a mutual appreciation for the prophet Abraham. We have a common history through Abraham. God promised blessings to Abraham's descendants, which includes Jews and Arabs, and in the New Testament all believers in Jesus are spiritual descendants of Abraham.

To be in agreement with God we must believe for blessings for both Jews and Arabs, who have lived side by side for thousands of years. Many today in the Western world consider Arabs to be anti-Semitic. Actually, Arabs are Semitic people. They are themselves descendants of Shem and Abraham. Anti-Semitism is a horrible sin. Sadly, the most horrible expressions of this sin have come from Europe. The Holocaust that killed six million Jews occurred in Europe. Those of European descent ought to be humble and not point fingers. We must all be on guard against anti-Semitism.

RESPECT FOR COMMON BELIEFS

We do well to respect that the Koran and the Bible agree on a number of accounts. Here are but a few of them:

- God created heaven and earth and made Adam and Eve;

- God accepted Abel's sacrifice, but rejected Cain's;

- God sent a flood and saved one family, the family of Noah;

- The Koran and the Bible speak of Abraham, Isaac, Ishmael, Jacob, Moses, David and a host of other prophets;

- God delivered Israel out of Egypt after each family had been told to sacrifice a lamb;

- God saved Lot from Sodom and Gomorrah;

- God gave the Psalms to David; and

- God sent John the Baptist (Yehya) to proclaim the coming Messiah.

We show respect by knowing the things we have in common.

RESPECT FOR COMMON VALUES

In addition to this, we Christians share many common values with Muslims. Born again believers in Jesus are concerned about the moral decay in society. Family breakup and abortion are issues where we stand shoulder to shoulder with Muslims. None of these common beliefs save us or make us righteous.

No, salvation is only found in Jesus. Yet, by being aware of these common beliefs, we demonstrate mutual respect. This is a far better approach than to use our Christian pulpits to speak derogatorily of others.

When I address a group of Muslim clerics or leaders I usually spend some time itemizing the things that we have in common. It is important to recognize that we are not complete strangers, not total opposites: we share certain values. Once I have shared these common values, I then begin to address our differences; which can be summarized in two sentences:

1. Gospel believers are unique because we believe Jesus is God revealed in the flesh;

2. Gospel believers are unique because we believe Jesus' death and resurrection put away all human sin and provides for our right standing before God.

These are truths we speak without compromise. If we approach Muslims in a narrow-minded, bigoted way that assumes they know nothing about Jesus or the holy prophets, this approach will only close doors. Instead, I respect peace-loving Muslims all over the world who sincerely try to serve God.

JESUS WILL SHOW HIMSELF

Ultimately my faith is in Jesus Himself. I encourage anyone of any religion to call on Jesus. You see, Jesus is unlike any other founder of a religion. Jesus is alive. When you call on Him with a sincere heart, He will answer you. If you ask Him to reveal Himself to you, He will, because "whoever calls on the name of the LORD shall be saved" (Romans 10:13) and "as many as received Him, to them He gave the right to become children of God, to those who believe in His name" (John 1:12).

Jesus cannot be isolated to one group of people. He did not come for Christians any more than He came for Muslims, Buddhists, Hindus or Shintoists. *Jesus is global.* This is the Gospel, "For God so loved the world that He gave His only begotten Son, that whoever believes in Him should not perish but have everlasting life. For God did not send His Son into the world to condemn the world, but that the world through Him might be saved" (John 3:16-17).

There is a great Gospel advantage. We do not have to win a debate. When any person calls on Jesus, he puts the Gospel to the test so to speak, and Jesus will reveal Himself to that person. Our Heavenly Father is very interested that every person will repent from self-reliance and self-righteousness and instead trust solely in what Jesus has done. God is patient; just like a farmer waits patiently for the harvest of the earth, so God waits patiently that many will receive His free gift of salvation provided through Jesus.

AN ILLUSTRATION FROM FOOTBALL

Let me illustrate from the world of sports. No sport has as great a global appeal as football (Americans call it soccer). I am writing this in Indonesia while the World Cup of football is on. Just this morning I saw Saudi Arabia and Tunisia play to a draw. People were flocking in front of every available TV set.

Imagine your country being in the World Cup Final game. Due to your excitement, not only do you purchase a ticket for yourself, but also for ten other special friends. You pay for everyone's tickets as well as plane travel and other expenses and everyone agrees to come to the game. On game day you find yourself in the stands, but the ten seats next to you are empty. The people whose tickets you paid for didn't bother to

show up. What a disappointment! You feel you have wasted
so much money.

God has provided a ticket to eternal life for every person on
planet earth. Jesus has removed the obstacle to eternal life,
which is our sin, by taking our sin upon Himself. Every person
has a seat reserved in heaven. God does not want empty seats,
but desires that His house would be full (Luke 14). This is
amazingly good news! God doesn't want anyone to perish, but
for all people to come to knowledge of the truth.

YOUR TICKET TO HEAVEN IS PAID

Your ticket to eternal life is provided. Jesus paid for it by His
death and resurrection. Come to Jesus! Call on Him, for as
many as receive Him, He gives the power to be God's children (John 1:12). Don't let your seat remain empty in God's
heaven.

This message may seem too good to be true. When you really
consider the implications you realize it is the only way that
anyone of us can have eternal life. No one is capable to live up
to God's commandments. There is not one righteous, no not
one (Romans 3:10). The only way to satisfy the requirements
of God, who is completely holy, is for us to be fully holy. This
is not humanly possible. Even those who do not fail outwardly
will sin in their thoughts or desires. That is why Jesus had to
come to be our substitute. He lived the perfect sinless life,
died for our sin, and rose again to give us life. Now, we have
the opportunity to receive the free gift of Jesus' righteousness.
When we call on Him for this gift, He is alive to save us. Call
on Jesus today!

PRAYER OF SALVATION

Heavenly Father, I come to You in the name of Jesus.
I believe that Jesus died for my sin, that He is alive.
With all of my heart and with my mouth I confess
"Jesus is Lord." Jesus come and live in me by Your
Holy Spirit. I receive this new life, and I repent
of trusting in my own good works and my own
abilities. From now on I only trust in Jesus and His
grace. Thank You God, in Jesus' name. Amen.

GLOSSARY

Abdullah: Muhammad's father, literal meaning –"servant of Allah."

Adam: The first man God created as recorded in the Bible and the Koran.

Ahl al Kitab: Arabic word meaning, People of the Book; term used to refer to Jews and Christians in the Koran.

Allah: Arabic word for "God," the Almighty. Linguistically it is related to the Hebrew name for God "Eloh," and the Aramaic, "Elah."

Bible: Literally means "books" - the New and Old Testament Scriptures as given by God to His prophets. Many references in this book (2 Corinthians, John, Acts etc.) are related to one of the 66 books in the Bible.

Born Again: Is a term used by Jesus to describe what happens when a person receives salvation and forgiveness of sins. Just like a person was once born naturally, when the Spirit of Jesus Christ comes to live inside of a person that individual is born spiritually.

Christ: "the Anointed One;" synonymous with Messiah.

Christian: There are two meanings, first in reference to an adherent of the religion of Christianity; secondly, in reference to a person who has been born again. A clear distinction is made between Christians who are followers of the religion, as compared to Christians who have a personal relationship with Jesus Christ (see Gospel Believer).

Christianity: The Christian religion. Though the word Christian was first mentioned some 30 to 40 years after Christ it took several generations for Christianity to be recognized as a religion. The early followers of Jesus did not focus on Christianity, but on the Gospel (see The Gospel).

Church: Common reference to a building that is used for the purpose of Christian teaching and prayer.

Church: In the Bible, this term is mostly used to describe a spiritual invisible body of believers, in reference to all those who have come to personal faith in Jesus Christ. It is possible to attend a church without being a part of the church; those who have been born again. (See "Born Again")

Covenant: An agreement between two parties; is used to describe God's agreement with mankind. A covenant between God and mankind always includes the giving of a life. This word is used in reference to the New Covenant and the Old Covenant, and applied interchangeably with the word "Testament" as in Old Testament and New Testament. The Old Covenant was given by God to Moses, and the New (and better) Covenant was given by God through Jesus Christ.

Crusades: A series of Christian invasions into the Middle East that began in 1099 AD and ended in 1270 AD.

Eternal Life: Synonymous with salvation. Eternal life begins now and continues forever in the presence of God (see Salvation).

God: English word for the Almighty.

[The] Gospel: Denotes the message of what God has done in Jesus for the whole world, through Jesus' death and resurrection.

Gospel Believer: An individual who has come to personal faith in The Gospel. Term is used to differentiate between a nominal Christian, who is an adherent to the traditions of the Christian religion and Gospel believer, one who has personally confessed Jesus as Lord. (See "Church")

Gospels: A term that includes the first four books of the New Testament of the Bible; Matthew, Mark, Luke and John. Each book is a description of what Jesus did and said.

Heaven: A literal place and specifically the place where believers in Christ will enjoy their eternal life.

Hell: A literal place originally intended for human habitation. Ultimate judgment regarding Hell will be given by God Himself.

Ibrahim: Arabic for Abraham.

Idul Adha: A Muslim holy day with a sacrifice of a cow, lamb, or goat in commemoration of Abraham's willingness to sacrifice his son.

Injel: The Arabic word for Gospel.

Isa [Esa]: The name for Jesus in the Koran.

Islam: The Arabic name for the religion practiced by Muslims.

John: One of Jesus' 12 disciples.

Koran: Islam's holy book, often spelled Qur'an.

Masih: "The Messiah," a term attributed to Jesus in the Koran and the Bible.

Masjid: The Arabic word for Mosque, literally "place of bowing."

Miracle: An act of God that transcends human ability.

Mosque: The English term for an Islamic house of worship.

Muhammad: (A.D. 570-632), the founder of Islam, and revered by Muslims as the "final prophet" from God.

Muslim: A follower of the religion of Islam.

Nasara: The Islamic term for Christian derived from the name Nazareth. In Arabic it is also related to the term for "helper" which is how the Koran views Jesus' disciples.

New Testament: The last 27 books of the Bible containing the fulfillment of that which was prophesied or foretold in the Old Testament. The New Testament can also be divided into two parts; the Gospels (history of what Jesus did and said) and the book of Acts and the Epistles (what Jesus is doing now after He has gone back to heaven). (See "Covenant")

Old Testament: The first 39 books of the Bible containing the Law, the Prophets and the history of the people of Israel. These writings predict and give details about the coming of Jesus. (See "Covenant")

Paul: The apostle who was given the task of revealing "the mystery" of what Jesus actually did at the cross. His assignment from God was particularly for the non-Jewish world. Jesus' revelation to Paul is found in the Book of Acts and the epistles of the New Testament.

Pharisees: Sect of Judaism, influential during Jesus' earthly ministry. The Pharisees arose as a "holiness" movement about 200 years before the birth of Jesus. They practiced an ultra legalistic form of Judaism, relying on their own performance and ability to obey God's commandments.

Redemption: "buy back," refers to Jesus' death being the price paid to buy mankind's freedom from the slavery of sin.

Redeemed: One who has experienced redemption.

Repentance: A total turn-around from reliance on self and one's own religious works and turning to reliance on what Jesus has done through His death and resurrection. The Bible calls it repentance from "dead works."

Righteousness: A state of right standing before God, which is impossible for humans to obtain by their own effort. The only righteousness acceptable to God is Jesus' sinless, perfect righteousness, available freely to all who believe in Him.

Salvation: Coming into right standing with God by believing in what Jesus did through His death and resurrection. Synonymous or similar words are "born again" and "eternal life."

Saved: Person who has experienced salvation by receiving Jesus' life and righteousness. This is different from being an adherent to the religion of Christianity. Being saved or having received salvation is supernatural. Jesus Himself imparts this new life into the saved person.

Shaytan: "to pull away from." In Arabic, "Satan."

Son of God: Does not denote God siring a son, an idea equally blasphemous to Muslims and Christians. The term is in reference to a spiritual relationship.

Son of Man: Term that describes Jesus' 33 year life in a limited human body, as well as His eternal work as a mediator between God and man.

Surah: Arabic word, meaning "gate" or "step-up." The name for a chapter in the Koran.

Yahya: The name in the Koran for John the Baptist.

Addressing Muslims after Friday prayer in a mosque.

'We can live with each other'

Minister of conservative Christian church pays exchange visit to Muslim mosque.

Newspaper clipping after a friendship visit to a mosque.

A moment of joy with Yaha Bin Salim Bega, blind for more than 30 years until Jesus healed him. (See front cover)

Gospel Festival in Tanga, East Africa – 95% of the population are Muslim.

Gospel Festival in Bandung, Indonesia, the world's largest Muslim nation

Gospel Festival in Sumatra, Indonesia

Gospel Festival in Quetta, Baluchistan, where 99% are Muslims

Karachi, Pakistan

In conversation with Pathan village
leaders on the border between
Pakistan and Afghanistan

Gospel Festival in Karachi, Pakistan where 96% are Muslims

Muslims rejoice as God's love in Jesus brought them healing

Pakistan

Here I receive typical Pathan clothing - a gift from Muslim friends

Muslim man healed out of his wheelchair

With Muslim leaders in Africa

91

CELEBRATING LIFE WITH JESUS

CELEBRATE
Jesus International

ABOUT THE AUTHOR

Passion for the unreached has taken Peter Youngren to more than 80 nations. He has led evangelistic Gospel Festivals with crowds of up to 600,000 attending a single service. In addition, over 246,000 pastors and leaders have attended his training seminars. Hundreds of Gospel workers are supported around the world on an ongoing basis. As founder of "Celebrate Jesus International," "Celebrate Magazine," "Celebrating Life with Jesus" TV program seen around the world, "Celebration Bible College" and the "Celebration Churches," Peter Youngren together with his wife RoxAnne, is committed to the Gospel reaching the entire earth.

Millions are reached via TV, literature and Gospel Festivals

Gospel Festival in the Horn of Africa

Celebrate Magazine highlights historic Gospel-advancing work taking place around the world. Enjoy amazing testimonies, challenging reports and insightful teaching.

To receive a free copy of our latest edition of Celebrate Magazine or for other products visit www.peteryoungren.org, call 1.905.646.0970 or 1.888.628.8241 (toll-free in North America). You can also contact our office. For the address, see back cover.

BOOK FAVORITES   www.peteryoungren.org/store

Salvation - God's Gift to You
More than 8 million in print! Order some today for unsaved loved ones or a coworker!
$US 2.⁹⁵

Triumph on the Enemy's Turf:
The Peter Youngren Story
Best-selling author Larry Keefauver wrote this biography sharing the triumphs and tragedies in ministry that have touched the world.
$US 11.⁰⁰

You Can Receive Healing From God
This classic demonstrates how anyone can successfully approach God to receive healing.
$US 14.⁹⁵

Blood Bought Victory
Take a fresh look at the power of Jesus' blood and how it affects your life!
$US 7.⁰⁰

The Final Sign
Find out why Jesus hasn't come back yet and what must happen before He does!
$US 12.⁹⁵

One Sacred Hour
Discover how every believer can participate in the Great Commission.
$US 5.⁹⁵

Fire From Heaven
This book documents the incredible story of fire evangelism in the former Soviet States.
$US 7.⁹⁵

Great Faith for Great Miracles
In this book you will discover the keys to the God-kind of faith. No more running on a treadmill chasing faith. Instead, faith will flow through you like the blood that flows through your veins.
$US 10.⁰⁰

Unlimited Faith (4cd)
This teaching will challenge and inspire you to enjoy the faith that moves the mountain every time.
$US 28.⁰⁰

Fabulous Good News (5cd)
A classic! This controversial teaching is sure to make you look at the scriptures again. Find keys to your destiny!
$US 35.⁰⁰

How Grace Works Amazingly in You (6cd) Only
God's grace produces holiness, maturity and miracles.
$US 42.⁰⁰

Faith That Works Through Him (3cd)
Connect with the Author and Finisher of your faith!
$US 21.⁰⁰

Enjoying God's Covenant of Favor (4cd) Discover how
God's unmerited favor brings increase to your life, family and ministry!
$US 28.⁰⁰

How to Live Life from the Inside Out (3cd)
Your inner life in Christ is hidden and waiting to be released.
$US 21.⁰⁰

Seven Priorities of Highly Effective People (4cd) A
study of the seven Hebrew Feasts.
$US 28.⁰⁰

It's All in the New Creation (4cd)
Discover how the new creation life releases a brand new "YOU."
$US 28.⁰⁰

Sit, Walk, Stand (4cd)
Three simple words take on a whole new perspective. An all-time classic!
$US 28.⁰⁰

The Exalted Jesus (3cd)
You have known the babe in the manger, the crucified Savior and the risen Lord. What about the exalted Jesus? Discover who Jesus is to you today.
$US 21.⁰⁰

The Gospel in Action
(5cd) 5 nights of miracle life in Guyana, South America. "I have never heard such authority in preaching" is a common remark about this series.
$US 35.⁰⁰

The Therapeutic Effects of the Cross
(4cd) There is so much more to the cross than you ever imagined. It works in and through us in an inter-personal relationship. Experience the therapy that only comes through the cross of Jesus!
$US 32.⁰⁰

When Life is Tough (4cd)
Discover how the reality of Christ in you can turn tombstones into stepping stones!
$US 28.⁰⁰

How to Change the Way You Think (3cd)
Change your thinking to God's thinking.
$US 21.⁰⁰

94

CELEBRATION BIBLE COLLEGE

FORMERLY WORLD IMPACT BIBLE INSTITUTE

Do you desire:

— to have God's anointing and fire within you?

— to build personal strength through the Holy Spirit?

— to be equipped for what God has planned for your future?

— to have a strong Bible foundation for your life and ministry?

— to expand and deepen your prayer life, Bible knowledge and understanding?

— to receive hands-on training within a vibrant, growing church and worldwide ministry?

If so, then Celebration Bible College is for you!

For a free information package please visit www.CelebrationBibleCollege.com
or call 1-888-942-4253 (North America) or +1-905-646-0970 (International)

CELEBRATION HOME BIBLE COLLEGE

THE Challenge - People want to study God's Word and are unable to attend the school as full-time students or unable to move to the Niagara Region.

THE Solution - Students can receive impartation as they study God's Word right in their own homes.

THE Way - Students receive the actual instruction presented in the Celebration Bible College classroom via DVD. The accompanying syllabus assists the student in following along with the DVD and absorbing the course material.

THE Program - Courses can be completed at the student's own pace. The DVDs are available for use in a four-month time frame similar to a CBC semester. Courses can be taken for spiritual growth, ministry training or leadership development. Celebration Bible College offers diplomas for one year, two year and three year programs.